Child Abuse

ISSUES
(previously Issues for the Nineties)

Volume 22

Editor

Craig Donnellan

Independence
Educational Publishers
Cambridge

First published by Independence
PO Box 295
Cambridge CB1 3XP
England

British Library Cataloguing in Publication Data
Child Abuse – (Issues Series)
I. Donnellan, Craig II. Series
362.7'6

ISBN 1 86168 054 6

Printed in Great Britain
City Print Ltd
Milton Keynes

Typeset by
Claire Boyd

Cover
The illustration on the front cover is by
The Attic Publishing Co.

CONTENTS

Chapter One: Abused Children

Chapter Two: Sex Offenders

Introduction

Child Abuse is the twenty-second volume in the series: **Issues**. The aim of this series is to offer up-to-date information about important issues in our world.

Child Abuse looks at the issues of child abuse and sex offenders.

The information comes from a wide variety of sources and includes:
Government reports and statistics
Newspaper reports and features
Magazine articles and surveys
Literature from lobby groups
and charitable organisations.

It is hoped that, as you read about the many aspects of the issues explored in this book, you will critically evaluate the information presented. It is important that you decide whether you are being presented with facts or opinions. Does the writer give a biased or an unbiased report? If an opinion is being expressed, do you agree with the writer?

Child Abuse offers a useful starting-point for those who need convenient access to information about the many issues involved. However, it is only a starting-point. At the back of the book is a list of organisations which you may want to contact for further information.

*****

Child sexual abuse

Information from Scottish Women's Aid

We all have contact with children and young people in different ways – as mothers, workers, relatives, neighbours, etc. It is important for parents and workers alike to have some understanding of the extent of sexual abuse, as well as information on the main issues such as why abuse happens, who abuses children, what we mean by child sexual abuse, why it is hard for children to tell, and how children try to tell us.

What is child sexual abuse?

Child sexual abuse is the abuse of power and trust over a child for the sexual gratification and pleasure of the adult. Child sexual abuse is emotional, physical, and sexual, and is usually perpetrated by an adult male.

Forms abuse takes:

Sexual – pornography, prostitution, rape, flashing, touching

Mental (emotional and psychological) – shutting away and not allowing light, isolation, constant criticism, sleep and food deprivation, manipulation and guilt creation, indecent phone calls, voyeurism (such as watching a child undress), referring or talking to the child in a sexual way, threats – whether or not the threats are carried out, forcing sexual display e.g. making child pose for pornographic pictures.

Physical – hitting/smacking, shaking, pushing, holding down, hair pulling, burning.

Abuse is intentional and creates fear, feelings of worthlessness and insecurity. Many children are also emotionally and/or physically abused 'separately' from the secret sexual abuse – they may be being emotionally abused through witnessing the abuse of their mother, and/or physically abused along with other members of the family.

It is important to identify other ways that children are abused, and which can further compound children's experience of sexual abuse – poverty and class, family structures, sexism, racism, heterosexism, and discrimination on the grounds of disability.

The law in Britain recognises the inability of children under 16 years old to give informed consent to sexual activity. It is a criminal offence for an adult to involve a child in any sexual act.

Sexual abuse is a crime which is usually committed in secret and may continue for many months/years. The abuse may begin with inappropriate touching and progress to more intrusive acts such as forced masturbation and rape.

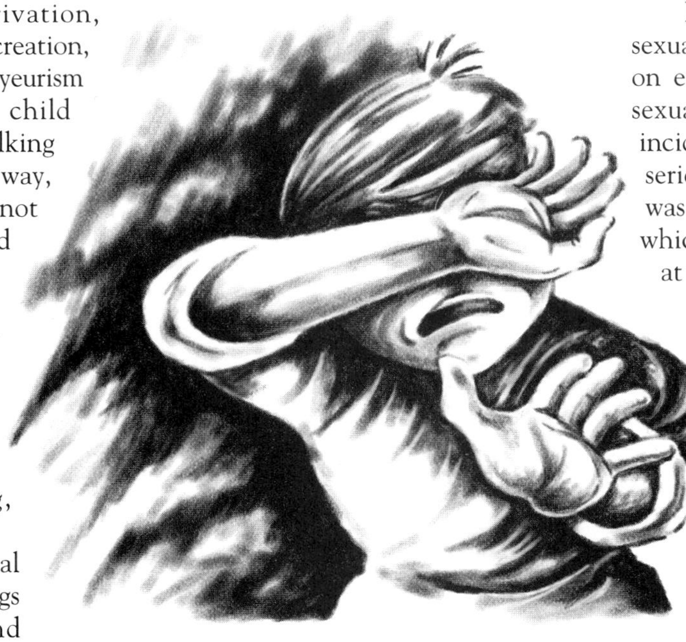

The prevalence of child sexual abuse

The most recent and comprehensive study of child sexual abuse in Britain undertaken by the University of North London showed that including any unwanted sexual event/interaction that occurred before age 18, over 1 in 2 females and 1 in 4 males had experienced at least one such event.

The most common form of sexual abuse was 'flashing' – which accounted for 27% of the experiences – the second most common was 'touching' which 23% of the people had suffered. If certain 'less serious' forms of abuse by peers, flashing, and abuse attempts which were successfully resisted are excluded the prevalence figures are 1 in 5 for women and 1 in 14 for men. The forms of abuse which more commonly result in prosecution, and which the general public associate with 'sexual abuse' (all forms of rape and forced masturbation) were experienced by 1 in 20 women and 1 in 50 men.

Definitions of what counts as sexual abuse have dramatic impacts on estimates of the prevalence of sexual abuse. To exclude certain incidents on the basis of a lack of seriousness or because the abuser was not an adult is to deny events which were defined as victimising at the time and which had serious long-term consequences.

• (Unless otherwise stated all prevalence figures in this section come from *An exploratory study of the prevalence of sexual abuse in a sample of 16-21 year olds* Kelly, Regan, Burton, Child and Woman Abuse Studies Unit, 1991.)

Survivors of abuse, women and children Women's Aid works with, and research, tell us that child sexual abuse is so common that without doubt some of the children and young people who come to Women's Aid and indeed to all agencies will have suffered sexual abuse. Because of the prevalence of child sexual abuse there will be children in every classroom, refuge, town, etc. who have been, are being, or will be subjected to child sexual abuse. We also know that abusive men can abuse both the woman and the children in various ways, together and separately – some men can use the emotional, physical and/or sexual abuse of the woman (and other members of the family) to cover up his secret and separate sexual abuse of the child.

Women whose children had been sexually abused talked to Janette Forman about how they themselves had been subjected to domestic abuse. (*Is There a Correlation Between Child Sexual Abuse and Domestic Violence?* Glasgow Women's Support Project). Amongst Janette's conclusions, and one supported by Women's Aid, is that woman protection is child protection. The fact that many women felt they had been dealt with punitively by agencies they went to for child protection reasons emphasises that the blame is not being targeted at the abuser, a fact which is detrimental to the child and the woman. Their strong testimonies and those of some of their children show that the woman is almost always the best source of support for the child, and of course hopefully *the* long-term support for the child – it is this relationship that we should be protecting. Children and women do not deserve to be abused, the abuser has the responsibility of society not to accept abuse and to put the blame firmly on the abuser, and to support and resource survivors of male abuse, including mothers of sexually abused children.

Who are the abusers?

Child sexual abuse is a crime most commonly committed by men against both girls and boys. The vast majority of abuse is committed by men – 95% of abusers are male. Women are between two and three times more likely to have experienced sexual abuse than men.

It is essential to realise that abuse is a gender issue, and is a result of the power imbalance within our society. At the same time it is vital to believe and support all survivors of sexual abuse which can be perpetrated by men, women, peers, and groups of people.

Children are more likely to be abused by someone they know and trust or by someone in authority than by a stranger. Abusers include: adults, parents, trusted adults/authority figures, other children, relatives, babysitters, neighbours, etc.

Children can be sexually abused at any age, from infancy to adolescence.

The sexual abuse of children occurs within every neighbourhood, class, racial background.

**** Scottish Women's Aid note***

Whilst the above applies, it is vital when considering the links between child abuse and domestic abuse to recognise that children are emotionally abused by living with domestic abuse and are also directly mentally and/or physically abused themselves. The abuser often continues the abuse of the woman and the child after separation through further contact with the child.

Studies asking where children are during attacks on their mothers have found that in 90% of cases the child is in the same or next room, a third of children try to intervene in attacks on their mothers, and perpetrators of domestic abuse physically abuse their children in 40-60% of cases where children are present in the home.

More details and information available from Scottish Women's Aid.

• The above is an extract from *Children – Equality and Respect*, produced by Scottish Women's Aid. See page 41 for address details.

Children's problems

In a record-breaking year, ChildLine answered 1,219,652 calls – more than ever before – and helped 102,816 children who contacted us for the first time last year – mainly by phone but also by letter.

Type of problem	Girls	Boys	Total	%
Bullying	11,224	3,087	14,311	14
Family relationship problem	10,947	2,219	13,166	13
Worries about others	9,544	1,014	10,558	10
Physical abuse	6,563	3,441	10,004	10
Sexual abuse	6,429	1,767	8,259	8
Facts of life	5,949	867	6,816	7
Pregnancy	6,314	351	6,665	6
Problem with friends	5,287	395	5,682	6
Partner relationship	3,954	441	4,395	4
School problem	1,417	494	1,911	2
Sexuality	952	896	1,484	2
Parents' divorce/separation	1,533	225	1,758	2
Runaway	1,049	583	1,630	2
Homelessness	689	565	1,254	1
Bereavement	1,040	146	1,186	1
Smoking	880	236	1,116	1
Depression/mental health	915	190	1,105	1
Health	889	171	1,060	1
Drug abuse	450	296	746	1
Loneliness	535	104	639	1
Eating problem	594	16	610	1
Suicide	447	88	535	1
Request for resources	392	133	525	1
Risk of abuse	435	88	523	1
Other*	5,041	1,473	6,514	6
Total	**83,530**	**19,286**	**102,816**	

This table refers to children contacting ChildLine for the first time in 1996/97. It does not include callers who first contacted us in a previous year, nor does it include adults who sought our help. It is based on calls both to the main 0800 1111 line and all other special lines. Some children ring several times; hence the difference between calls answered and children counselled. Percentages have been rounded up or down to the nearest whole figure and therefore do not total precisely 100 per cent.

* The category entitled 'other' includes problems which individually added up to less than one per cent of the total – such as children who called about alcohol problems, self-harm, racism and cultural or religious problems, solvent abuse and worries about unemployment.

Source: ChildLine

Fact or fiction?

Like most people, you have probably heard or read a lot of stories about child abuse in the news lately. But how much do you really know about it? Test yourself on this quiz.

Decide which of the statements printed in bold are true and which are false. But try to make up your mind before reading the answers! Why not ask your partner or friend to do the quiz too, and compare your answers?

If a child is abused it won't make a lot of difference in the long run, as they won't remember much about it when they grow up.

False. Abuse can ruin a child's life. Younger children are likely to remember less about the experience, but the emotional and psychological effects may be even more damaging.

Children who have been abused may grow up feeling that they are worthless and may have difficulty forming happy relationships. Research has shown that they may also be more likely to turn to alcohol, drugs or crime, and may be more likely to abuse their own children.

It's not only poor parents from deprived backgrounds who abuse their children.

True. People who abuse children come from all social backgrounds, all walks of life, and different races and cultures. They can be parents, or other people the child knows well, like a family friend or close relative. (Only in one in every six or seven cases is the abuser a total stranger.)

Child abuse is very rare. It's just the press that blows the problem out of all proportion.

False. No one knows exactly how common child abuse is, but the number of cases reported and the number of children receiving help are increasing every year. The NSPCC estimates that between 150 and 200 children die every year in

NSPCC

England and Wales following incidents of abuse or neglect. Many incidents of abuse are never reported, but we know that three to four children die each week following abuse and neglect. The media have helped to make people aware of the problem, and this may be one reason why more cases of child abuse are being reported.

It is illegal for children under 13 to be left alone at home, for example while their parents go out for the evening.

False. There is no law which states the age at which children can be left unsupervised. But parents can be prosecuted for neglect if they leave children who are too young to look after themselves and something happens to the child in their absence. Ideally, all babysitters should be 16 or over, because children under 16 cannot be held legally responsible for anything that happens to a child in their care.

Always try to make sure that your babysitter or child-minder is reliable and trustworthy, and listen to your instincts if you have any doubts about the person.

It is all right for fathers to hug and kiss their children – boys as well as girls – and for them to bath children too young to bath themselves.

True. All the news about sexual abuse cases recently has made some fathers worried about showing affection for their children. All these activities are perfectly normal and healthy. Children need to be shown warmth and affection by their fathers as well as their mothers.

It is only sexual abuse if a parent uses a child to satisfy his or her own sexual desires.

'A good hiding never did anyone any harm.'

False. Adults who were physically punished when they were children sometimes say that it didn't do them any harm. But although we may not realise the connection between a bad experience in our childhood and the feelings and difficulties we may have as adults, the connection will certainly be there.

Smacking is not the best way to discipline a child.

True. Children need limits to be set to their behaviour, but punishing them with angry or aggressive actions is not the most effective way of doing this. It may not even make the child behave any differently and will not teach them respect or self-control. It is better to find positive ways of setting limits. For example, if children are used to love and praise, they will be upset by your disappointment and unsmiling face. With younger children you can usually distract their attention to something else.

Shouting at your children can't possibly be a form of child abuse.

False. You may well need to shout at a child sometimes – particularly if they are in immediate danger. But if you are constantly shouting and criticising, a child will feel unloved, and will feel that they can 'never do anything right'. Eventually they may become withdrawn or develop other long-term behaviour problems.

World states tackle spiralling child sex abuse

Swedish congress against exploitation of minors aims to outrage, as California leads way with tough penalties. By Jon Henley in Stockholm

The numbers are estimates, but if they even approach the truth they are horrifying. Almost no corner of the world, from the poorest backstreet of Latin America to the ritziest European capital, can claim to be immune.

There are 70,000 child prostitutes in Zambia, 200,000 in Thailand, 40,000 in Venezuela, 25,000 in the Dominican Republic and 500,000 in India. In America, between 100,000 and 300,000 children are sexually exploited through prostitution and pornography every year.

Girls of 12 have been found selling themselves on the streets of Britain; the Netherlands is thought to have 1,000 child sex workers.

In eastern Europe the situation is acute: even Estonia, with a population a quarter the size of London's, employs 1,500 minors, some as young as 10, in its fledgling sex industry.

As delegates from 122 countries gathered in Stockholm yesterday for the first World Congress on the Commercial Sexual Exploitation of Children, the research they brought with them revealed the staggering scale of child sex abuse.

'The commercial sexual exploitation of children has become a global, multi-billion-dollar industry,' Carol Bellamy, executive director of Unicef, said in her opening speech to the conference. 'Manifestations vary from society to society, but it takes place in virtually every country – and it appears to be booming.'

The effects of sexual exploitation on children are profound and often permanent, Ms Bellamy said. 'Normal development is compromised, self-esteem and confidence are undermined. The vast majority of sexually exploited children are denied their right to education. Many are ostracised by their families and communities.'

The actor Roger Moore, who is attending the conference, stressed the need for abused children not to feel guilty. During an interview in which he said he had been a victim of childhood abuse, he said: 'They are being exploited. We have to tell them that.'

> ***'Manifestations vary from society to society, but it takes place in virtually every country – and it appears to be booming'***

He said he had been too ashamed of the incident to tell anyone until he was 16. 'I felt I had done something wrong. I had done absolutely nothing wrong at all.'

Experts say many factors lie behind the recent global rise of child sex abuse. In some societies, the drive towards western-style consumerism has combined, disastrously, with traditional beliefs that young children, particularly girls, are property to be traded – families simply sell their children for something they want more.

Fear of AIDS increasingly leads men to seek ever younger prostitutes, in the mistaken belief that they are safer. And modern technology – the video camera, home editing suite, computer graphics and the Internet – has made it easier for paedophiles to produce and exchange child pornography, and far more difficult for police to stop them.

Organisers admit the five-day congress, sponsored by the Swedish government in co-operation with Unicef and non-governmental groups, is unlikely to produce many concrete, immediate changes, but it aims to produce more than well-meaning words.

Tom Tscherning, one of the organisers and a former Swedish ambassador, said the congress should increase international co-operation aimed at strengthening and harmonising legislation. 'Laws are the ultimate protection for children,' he said. 'Nowhere near enough is being done either to make laws sufficiently strong or to enforce them when they are in place.'

Australia has led the way in extra-territorial legislation which allows its nationals to be prosecuted at home for sex crimes against children committed abroad.

Of the 12 countries which have adopted similar laws, Australia has by far the highest rate of action and the most severe penalties, including jail terms of up to 17 years, according to a Bangkok-based group, ECPAT (End Child Prostitution, Child Pornography And the Trafficking of Children for Sexual Purposes).

By contrast, Sweden is almost alone among European countries in failing to pass legislation outlawing the possession of child pornography. Swedish campaign groups have threatened to disrupt the conference, and the anomaly – caused by constitutional procedure – has been attacked by the Swedish queen.

If nothing else, the congress should produce a 'real sense of outrage', Ron O'Grady of ECPAT said in his opening remarks. 'Because basically, if we accept a world in which children can be bought and sold as if they were goods in a supermarket, we forfeit the right to call ourselves civilised.'

Britain sought to take the lead yesterday in the battle against child prostitution.

The junior Home Office minister, Timothy Kirkhope, speak-ing at the Stockholm summit, was due to urge all countries to adopt their own action plans, as well as to commit themselves to extradite people accused of committing sex offences in other countries and to prosecute offenders in their own countries.

Mr Kirkhope planned to use the gathering to highlight Britain's measures to combat the sexual abuse of children. Measures to enable British 'sex tourists' to be prosecuted in Britain are expected in the autumn.

He will also offer practical assistance. British detectives have been consulted by police investigating the Belgian child sex scandal, and the Metropolitan Police helped run a training programme in the Philippines to improve child protection programmes.

Australian's '850 crimes'

An Australian man, aged 75, appeared in court yesterday charged with 850 child sex crimes in Australia, after earlier this year being charged with committing similar offences in Bangkok.

The man, whose name cannot be released for legal reasons, faces charges of indecent dealing, sodomy and permitting sodomy with eight children between the 1960s and 1980s.

The children were aged between 13 and 16 at the time of the alleged offences, the Brisbane magistrates court heard. Police said they expected more charges.

In May, the same man became the second Australian charged with sex offences against children in an overseas country, the court was told.

On that occasion he was charged with two counts of sexual conduct involving a child aged under 16, and one of possessing four rolls of film depicting child abuse acts. It was alleged he had had sex with a girl and a boy in Bangkok between 1994 and 1995. – Reuter.

Briton held in Albanian jail

Albanian authorities have arrested a British man and charged him with sexually abusing two young boys, a Tirana prosecutor said yesterday.

The prosecutor, Adnan Xhelili, said Paul Thompson, aged 34, from Wiltshire, was arrested on Sunday in a hotel in the Adriatic resort of Durres, 30 miles west of Tirana.

Mr Thompson, who is in jail, denies the charges. He could face up to five years in prison if convicted.

Mr Xhelili said Mr Thompson, who is divorced, said he had befriended the boys, both aged under 10, because they reminded him of his own children who live with his former wife in London.

The prosecutor's office said no date had been set for a trial as inquiries were under way. The British embassy said an official had gone to visit Mr Thompson.

The age of consent for both heterosexual and homosexual sex in Albania is 14. Many destitute children can be seen begging in the streets. – Reuter.

Repeat offenders face 'castration'

Drummon Ayres in Los Angeles

Taking the lead in a nationwide push to enact tougher sex-crime laws in America, California is set to pass a measure requiring 'chemical castration' of repeat child molesters.

The measure mandates that any child-sex offender convicted twice be periodically injected, after release from prison, with a drug that inhibits sex drive – unless the offender voluntarily submits to surgical castration.

A first-time child molester convicted of a particularly bad offence would have to undergo the same treatment.

The bill is expected to be passed this week and will then face constitutional challenges.

Supporters of the measure, who say it will protect some of society's most vulnerable crime targets, do not consider it too punitive, given the severity of the crime and the often compulsive, recidivistic and unrepentant nature of offenders.

'What we're up against is the kind of criminal who, just as soon as he gets out of jail, will immediately commit this crime again at least 90 per cent of the time,' said Bill Hoge, the chief sponsor of the bill.

'So why not give these people a shot to calm them down and bring them under control or, alternatively, give them the option of going under the knife? That's what they do in some countries in Europe, like Sweden and Denmark and Germany. And when they do – medicine or surgery – the repeat rate drops to 2 per cent.'

Opponents of the bill say it is a simplistic overreaction to a complex problem.

'This measure raises some very, very serious constitutional questions, not to mention medical questions,' said Valerie Small Navarro of the American Civil Liberties Union.

'There are problems regarding the right to privacy, the right to procreate, the right to control over one's body. There are questions about drug side effects and whether treatment will work in every case, especially if it isn't voluntary and isn't accompanied by therapy and counselling, which the bill doesn't mandate.' – *New York Times*.

If you care about children . . .

A guide to understanding child abuse

Some abused children speak out

'My dad told me that it was normal for him to have sex with me. Because he was my dad, I had to believe him. He wants me to do all sorts of sexual things. Please help. I don't want my dad to go to jail. I just want it to stop.'

Girl, aged 13

'My mother shouted at me practically all the time. Once she lashed out at me. She shook me violently and really frightened me. She would turn me out of the house in the middle of the night. Sometimes she kept me away from school – she wanted me to stay home and do errands for her. I don't think she'll ever admit that she's got a problem.'

Girl, aged 15

'My dad was angry with me and sent me to bed. I wanted to go to the toilet but I didn't dare. In the end I wet the bed. When my dad found out he pulled me out of bed. "You dirty little devil", he shouted. He pulled me by my hair into the bathroom.'

Boy, aged 8

What every child needs

Respect
Your child's idea of what is important may be very different from yours. Try to remember this when your child wants to tell you something urgently, even if you are busy.

Physical care
This includes warmth, adequate clothing and enough to eat.

Praise
This will help children to grow up to be secure, confident adults.

Attention
Listen to children: not just to their words, but to anything they might be trying to tell you in their behaviour.

Trust
Make sure that your children know that you trust them and that you will always believe and help them.

Love
This is the most vital need of all.

'My role as a mother is the most important I've ever had. Being a parent isn't easy, but even when things get on top of you, you know that your children just love you for who you are, and it makes everything worthwhile.'

Actress Lynda Bellingham

What can you do?

Most parents and other adults want to meet children's needs. Here are some ways in which you may be able to help children to avoid abuse and to grow up happily.

- If a child tells you that he or she has been abused, it is important that you believe the child and take action straight away. The sooner you take action, the more likely it is that abuse will stop and the child will recover from his or her experiences.
- If you know someone who you think may be abusing a child, try to share your worry first with someone who knows the family, like a relative or neighbour, or the child's teacher or school nurse. If you are still worried, please do not hesitate to contact the NSPCC Child Protection Helpline (see How the NSPCC can help) or the Social Services Department of your local authority. You do not have to give your name, though you will be encouraged to, in case you can provide further information which could help the child later on.
- If you yourself are abusing a child or are in danger of doing so, please ask for help immediately. You could ring the NSPCC Child Protection Helpline and talk to a counsellor.

Many people may feel reluctant to report a suspected case of child

Photo: NSPCC / Naomi Schillinger. Posed by models.

abuse, because they fear that the offender will be sent to prison or the child taken away from home. This is not necessarily the case. In fact, the NSPCC strives to work with the whole family, to prevent the abuse continuing and to keep the family together. But in a small number of cases, where it is felt that the child will not be safe, a child may have to be removed from the home. The vast majority of these children return home as soon as it is felt that they will be safe.

How the NSPCC can help

The NSPCC is a charity which exists to prevent child abuse and protect children. It provides a number of services to help families.

NSPCC Child Protection Helpline (0800 800 500)

This is a free, 24-hour telephone helpline for anyone worried about a child who may be in danger. The helpline can organise investigations if you are worried that a child may be suffering abuse, and also offers advice and counselling. The helpline is open to both adults and children.

Child protection teams and projects

The NSPCC has a network of Child Protection Teams and Projects covering England, Wales and Northern Ireland. The teams are staffed by trained social workers. Team members work closely with the police and social services to help abused children and their families.

Counselling and support

The NSPCC Child Protection Helpline helps parents who feel they are in danger of abusing their children, and offers counselling to adults who were abused as children.

Raising awareness

We campaign to change attitudes towards children and keep the issue of child abuse in the public eye.

To find out more about child abuse issues and how the NSPCC can help, please send for some of our other publications.

• The above is an extract from *If you care about children . . .*, produced by the NSPCC. See page 41 for address details.

Sexual exploitation

Richard Morris reports on the experience of a former rent boy on the streets of London and on some of the steps taken to combat the sexual exploitation of children

Two years ago Jason Douglas brought out his first novel to wide coverage and wide acclaim. An on the road story about two friends travelling stickily through Britain on holiday, it is a precisely outlined, sometimes irritatingly detailed portrait of two men.

One of them is coming to terms with a miserable past including being abused as a child, while the other doesn't seem to be thinking about much at all, except where to find the next medieval cathedral. It is a strong, patchy, acerbic and moving work, stylistically inventive, emotionally honest and uncompromising.

It draws heavily on Jason's heightened awareness of the dark side of life, a recurrent note in all he does. That he has a suspicious attitude towards the world stems from what he endured in his youth. Brought up in Ayrshire he ran away from home at the age of 13 and slept at various doss-houses until he reached London where he met Simon the day he arrived at Euston Station. He offered Jason a roof over his head and friendship. Within a week he was on the streets as a rent boy and lasted the circuit three years before returning to Scotland to try to begin a new life. Happily he succeeded. Others aren't as fortunate.

The two men in his book reflect his two lives. The happy-go-lucky one is the person he wanted to be and still does; the other is the person he is. It is a tainted biographical account of his three years hanging around King's Cross and Piccadilly Circus selling his body to tourists.

> ***'It is essential that there is effective action both nationally and internationally to combat the scourge of child exploitation and sex tourism'***

'When the time is right I shall hold up my hand and say "this was me". But my wife is the only one who knows. I still feel guilty and this was 20 years ago. A lot of clients I met on the streets regularly went overseas for sex because they knew few controls existed and younger rent boys and children were available with no questions asked.

'There has to be workable aid and to my mind that does not stop at offering to take down cultural and legal barriers, it means providing financial help as well to assist educational, employment and social schemes.'

At the recent World Congress on the Commercial Sexual Exploitation of Children held in Stockholm, the UK Government, represented by Home Office minister Timothy Kirkhope, was loudly applauded for its tougher stance and its three-point plan that included the proposals that all countries should extradite offenders who commit sexual offences against children

and that firmer action is taken against those who take part in sex holidays abroad.

The day before presenting the Government's report, Kirkhope said: 'It is essential that there is effective action both nationally and internationally to combat the scourge of child exploitation and sex tourism.

'The UK leads the world in the action it has taken to protect young people and to catch and punish the evil people who take part in these disgusting practices. Each country has its own culture and criminal justice system. What works in one country may not work elsewhere. But it is important that we all learn from each other and adopt one another's best practice.'

The 1995 Howard Hughes rape and murder of 7-year-old Sophie Hook in Wales and other sex-related killings prompted more than one newspaper to call for convicted paedophiles to be publicly listed on a national register and the Home Secretary is considering the idea.

One evening newspaper, the *Evening Echo* in Bournemouth, has pre-empted the possibility of the Government compiling a list by producing its own. Every month the *Echo* publishes the names, addresses, ages and details of newly convicted Dorset paedophiles, as well as reporting cases as they come up in the courts, whether in Britain or overseas, that include offenders who have some local connection.

'The UK leads the world in the action it has taken to protect young people and to catch and punish the evil people who take part in these disgusting practices'

The police too are anxious that more is done to counter the increase in child abuse cases. The Government has supported the Sexual Offences (Conspiracy and Incitement) Act 1996 which extends the jurisdiction of British courts over conspiracies and incitement to commit sexual offences against children outside of the UK and to allow trials of those who abuse children to be tried in this country. However, legal experts such as barrister Andrew Carter QC, a specialist in criminal law, point out the difficulties in gathering sufficient evidence and witnesses from abroad and warns that this could delay legal action and might well cancel it out altogether.

'To mount a satisfactory prosecution in the UK might be quite difficult. Extradition in itself is no longer a problem, only Belgium and Estonia have yet to ratify the European Convention on Extradition and most other countries in the world are extradition partners, but getting witnesses to come to Britain to testify would be a lot more difficult. We have to develop a system which is a lot easier to operate.'

The 1996 Act aims to catch tour operators who organise travel abroad for child molesters and groups of individuals who might plan to turn their holiday into a sexual fantasy involving young children. The Association of British Travel Agents (ABTA) regularly conducts spot-checks on travel operators' brochures to ensure that they comply with ABTA standards, but rarely does it check package holiday destinations in countries known to have an active commercial child sex trade.

But Britain is leading the way with gathering intelligence on child abusers. The Paedophile Intelligence section of the National Criminal Intelligence Service (NCIS) monitors those involved in child sexual abuse and child pornography to help agencies throughout the world, and the Metropolitan Police has in the past organised a training course in the Philippines to help improve child protection programmes.

'Stockholm and the awful atrocities in Belgium and incidents in the UK have put the sexual exploitation of children at the top of the world's agenda. We can only hope that it stays there,' adds Carter, 'for the sake of the world's children.'

Protecting children everywhere against commercial sexual exploitation

'If we accept a world in which children can be bought and sold as if they are goods in a supermarket, we forfeit the right to call ourselves civilised.'

Ron O'Grady, Chair of ECPAT International

What is the commercial sexual exploitation of children?

It happens to children world-wide. It is the sexual abuse of a child by an adult paid for either by cash or in kind (through meals, clothes, payment of rent etc.). The three main elements are:

a) child prostitution

b) child pornography

c) the trafficking and sale of children for sexual purposes.

Why should we take action?

- Because Britons are amongst those who sexually exploit children overseas.
- Prostitution is a death sentence for many children. STDs (sexually transmitted diseases) and AIDS/HIV, to which children are more susceptible, are rampant in the sex industries.

ecpat (uk)
END CHILD PROSTITUTION PORNOGRAPHY TRAFFICKING

- Children suffer tremendous physical and emotional pain as a result of prostitution.
- Prostituted children are victims not criminals.
- Every child, however poor, has the right not to be treated as a sexual commodity.

Who are the children?

They are both boys and girls aged up to 18 years, though the majority are girls. They generally come from poor, rural families or are homeless children living on the streets. Many are sold by family or friends, tricked or abducted into prostitution. Some children may simply have no other option but to prostitute themselves in order to survive.

Why are children sexually exploited?

The root causes are complex. Poverty, lack of opportunities for education or employment, homelessness, criminal networks and family breakdown are all important factors. Children from minority ethnic groups are particularly vulnerable, as are girls who are often seen as less 'important' than boys. Children are also increasingly seen as commodities in a global market who can be bought or sold.

What is ECPAT (UK)?

ECPAT (UK) is part of an international network of ECPAT groups in over 30 countries, we were set up by a number of agencies already working on children's rights.

ECPAT stands for End Child Prostitution, Child Pornography And the Trafficking of Children for Sexual Purposes.

What does ECPAT (UK) do?

ECPAT (UK) aims to:

- raise awareness amongst the British public on the international aspects of the commercial sexual exploitation of children

- encourage UK citizens and organisations to take action on the international aspect of the commercial sexual exploitation of children.

We campaign on the following key areas:

Laws:
We lobby Governments including the British Government and the European Union to strengthen laws protecting children and to enforce those laws. We want children everywhere to be protected from British sex offenders.

Tourism:
We inform the travelling public of the steps they can take as individuals both at home and overseas to help prevent the commercial sexual exploitation of children.

Codes of practice:
We want companies, the tourism industry and the military to develop codes of good practice so British staff overseas will understand the issues, will be aware of the laws and will take action to protect children.

We work with children's chari-ties and aid agencies, the tourism industry, MPs, the UK Government, the European Union, trade unions and individual supporters.

'The commercial sexual exploitation of children is an outrage. ECPAT (UK)'s campaign has brought this issue to the forefront of the public's attention.'
Jon Snow, Newscaster

ECPAT (UK) and our supporters have already successfully lobbied for a new law that will allow the prosecution in the UK of British nationals and residents who commit sexual offences against children whilst overseas.

In 1996 ECPAT (UK) received a Media Natura One World Award for best public information campaign by an NGO.

Our successful campaign has been built on . . . letter writing campaigns . . . petitions . . . postcards . . . conferences . . . exhibitions . . . events.

How you can help . . .

- Become a supporter and receive our newsletters and updates on regular action you can take. We have publications, videos and reports on all aspects of the commercial sexual exploitation of children. For an annual supporter subscription please send £2.50 to cover mailing costs (make cheques payable to ECPAT UK).
- Make a donation to ECPAT (UK) or to a project working with children overseas – contact us for more details.
- Take action: contact us at the address on page 41.

Why children call ChildLine

Eighteen per cent of children contacting us for the first time in 1996/7 (18,263) did so because they had been sexually or physically abused, or both, and many others mentioned having been abused when they called us about another problem – such as feeling suicidal, or having run away from home.

Sexual abuse

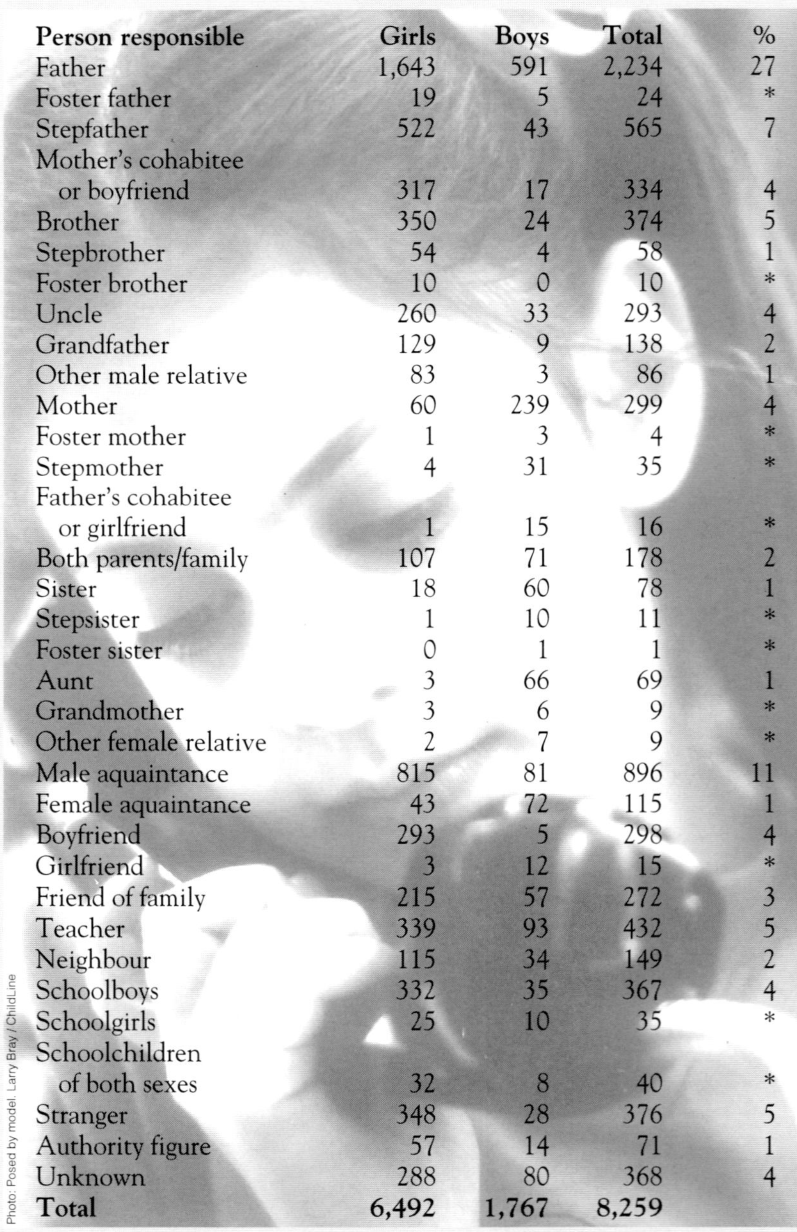
Photo: Posed by model. Larry Bray / ChildLine

Person responsible	Girls	Boys	Total	%
Father	1,643	591	2,234	27
Foster father	19	5	24	*
Stepfather	522	43	565	7
Mother's cohabitee or boyfriend	317	17	334	4
Brother	350	24	374	5
Stepbrother	54	4	58	1
Foster brother	10	0	10	*
Uncle	260	33	293	4
Grandfather	129	9	138	2
Other male relative	83	3	86	1
Mother	60	239	299	4
Foster mother	1	3	4	*
Stepmother	4	31	35	*
Father's cohabitee or girlfriend	1	15	16	*
Both parents/family	107	71	178	2
Sister	18	60	78	1
Stepsister	1	10	11	*
Foster sister	0	1	1	*
Aunt	3	66	69	1
Grandmother	3	6	9	*
Other female relative	2	7	9	*
Male aquaintance	815	81	896	11
Female aquaintance	43	72	115	1
Boyfriend	293	5	298	4
Girlfriend	3	12	15	*
Friend of family	215	57	272	3
Teacher	339	93	432	5
Neighbour	115	34	149	2
Schoolboys	332	35	367	4
Schoolgirls	25	10	35	*
Schoolchildren of both sexes	32	8	40	*
Stranger	348	28	376	5
Authority figure	57	14	71	1
Unknown	288	80	368	4
Total	**6,492**	**1,767**	**8,259**	

Speaking out about abuse

What every young person should know

Dear Anita

Anita Naik, Problem columnist, *Just Seventeen* magazine

No one understands

Please help me. I'm 15 years old and will be taking my GCSEs this year. My problem is that I can't concentrate on anything because I feel so unhappy and depressed. I just want to hide myself away and cry most of the time, but I don't know why. My mum never really listens to me. She just doesn't want to know about my problems and keeps telling me not to be so stupid. I can't talk to my mates about it because they'd think I'm weird.

Gary, aged 15, Nottingham

Don't despair Gary. You're certainly not weird – or alone! Lots of people feel depressed without knowing exactly why – especially during adolescence. With exams looming and important decisions to make about your future, this is bound to be a stressful time for you. The best solution is to talk through your worries with an adult you trust. If your parents won't listen, then try talking to a close relative or a sympathetic teacher at school. You may find it easier to talk to someone on a helpline. You can ring ChildLine or the NSPCC Child Protection Helpline (see Are you all right? on the next page).

I feel dirty

I just don't know what to do. I'm 14 and my dad is making me have sex with him. Sometimes I feel angry and confused, and at other times I feel dirty and ashamed. I want to tell my mum but I'm afraid that she won't believe me. Please please help me. I'm really desperate. I feel very confused because in some ways I love my dad, and I don't want him to go to prison. I just want the abuse to stop.

Anne, aged 14, Birmingham

NSPCC

I understand how bad you must be feeling. Remember, you are not to blame in any way for what has happened to you. Please tell your mum what has been going on, as soon as you can. If you feel you can't tell your mum, or you try and she doesn't believe you, then tell another adult you trust. You may find it helpful to talk to ChildLine or the NSPCC Child Protection Helpline (see Are you all right? on the next page). You will probably need help to overcome your experiences. Your dad won't necessarily be sent to prison, though he will need help to understand that what he has done is wrong. In time, you may well be able to rebuild your relationship with him.

They make my life hell

I used to like school, up until a few months ago. There's a gang of three girls in the fifth form who've started to pick on me and they're making my life hell. Every time I see them they ask me to lend them money. If I say I don't have any, they start pushing me around and calling me names (I'm quite small). And it seems to be just me they pick on. Should I tell my teacher, or will that make things worse?

Corrine, aged 12, London

I know how cruel and upsetting this kind of bullying can be, and these girls need to be stopped. It's easy to be tough when there are three of you against one. Do you have friends who would help you confront these girls in public? Tell the bullies what cowards they are, and that you will tell their teacher what is going on unless they stop their threats. If you feel you can't do this, then you should tell your parents or the adult you live with, and ask your teacher for help right away. Most teachers are used to handling this sort of problem and should be able to stop these girls without making it difficult for you. You may also wish to ring ChildLine who receive many calls about bullying (see Are you all right? on the next page).

I feel ashamed

About two years ago when my mum was in hospital, a good friend of my mum and dad used to come round to look after me until dad got home from work. I've never told anyone this before, but he used to bring round girlie magazines and get me to look at them with him. He said it was normal for boys my age to do this. Once he made me touch his penis and tried to touch mine. He told me to keep it a special secret. I can't keep this secret any more. I feel ashamed about what happened, but don't know what to do.

Tim, aged 13, Devon

It's not you who should feel ashamed. By showing you pornographic pictures and asking you to touch his penis, this so-called 'friend' committed sexual abuse, which is a criminal offence. He betrayed your parents' trust and took advantage of you. He asked you to keep it a secret so that he wouldn't be caught. I suggest you tell your parents or someone you trust exactly what you've told me. If they don't believe you, please don't give up, but keep telling another trusted adult until someone does. I realise this may not be easy, especially as the abuser is a family friend. This man may be abusing someone else, so he must be stopped – now. There are free helplines that offer support and advice for young people who have been abused. You can ring ChildLine or the NSPCC Child Protection Helpline (see Are you all right? below). Or your parents may want to contact the social services or the NSPCC for help (see What happens next? Below).

Protect yourself

If you have to walk alone after dark, choose a busy, well-lit route. And never take short-cuts through parks or secluded areas.

Trust your instincts about people you meet. If you're in any doubt, don't go off with them, particularly if you will be alone.

If someone attacks you in any way, it is OK to shout, kick, bite and do anything that will help you to escape.

If anyone tries to pressurise you into sexual activity, or wants to make you do things which do not feel right, you have a right to tell them not to – even if the person is someone you know and love.

Are you all right?

If you think that you are being abused, or you have feelings or difficulties which you think may be related to having been abused when you were younger, please talk to an adult you trust, or ring a helpline.

Talk to an adult

It is almost impossible for a young person to stop abuse or recover from it without involving an adult. Try and find the words to tell an adult you trust what is happening. If you can't find the words, try writing something down and practise saying it, or ask a friend to help. If the adult you tell doesn't believe you, keep telling until someone does.

Ring a helpline

You can call either of the helplines below free of charge, at any time of the day or night. You can call from any phone, including a public telephone. If you can't get through straight away, please keep trying. Helplines can also help you work out who to tell and how to tell them, and can put you in touch with organisations which can help you.

NSPCC Child Protection Helpline
Telephone: 0800 800 500

This helpline is for young people and children as well as parents and other adults. You can ring if you

Photo: Sandra Lousada / NSPCC. Posed by model

think you are being abused yourself, or if you are worried about a friend or any other young person or child. The NSPCC will offer advice and take any necessary action to stop the abuse.

ChildLine
Telephone: 0800 1111
This helpline is for young people and children, and can help with any kind of problem, including abuse. You can also ring them if you are worried that a friend is being abused. If you don't want to phone you can write to them at: Freepost 1111, London N1 0BR. You do not need a stamp.

Kidscape
Telephone: 0171 730 3300
You can ring Kidscape for information on how you can beat bullying. A special bullying counsellor is available on Tuesdays and Wednesdays, between 9.30am and 4.30pm. Or write for a free leaflet, enclosing a SAE, to: 152 Buckingham Palace Road, London SW1W 9TR.

What happens next?

When you tell an adult about serious abuse, he or she may have to involve other people to help you sort things out. Usually there will be a social worker, and sometimes a police officer and doctor. What happens next is called an 'investigation'. In order to help you, these professionals will ask you questions to find out exactly what happened. These questions may be embarrassing or difficult. But the adults involved are used to talking to young people who have had similar experiences, and should make it as easy as possible for you. As part of the investigation, the professionals will probably also speak to your family and other people who know you well. After the investigation there may be a 'case conference' where the professionals will meet and make decisions about how best to help you. You might be able to go along to all or part of the case conference.

During the investigation and case conference, it is important that you make sure that the professionals know how you feel. Try not to be afraid to ask questions, and let them know how they could make things easier for you.

Young people who have been abused are only taken away from home if it is felt that it is dangerous for them to stay. The majority stay in their own home. Most of those who are removed return home just as soon as it is felt that they will be safe.

If you would like to find out more about investigations and case conferences, and how to cope with them, please write to the NSPCC for a copy of our booklet called *Child abuse investigations: A guide for children and young people*. (Our address is on page 41 of this book.)

What is child abuse?

Abuse occurs when adults hurt children or young people under 18, either physically or in some other way. Usually the adult is someone the child or young person knows well, such as a parent, relative, or friend of the family.

There are four main kinds of abuse:

Physical abuse
Physical abuse includes hitting, kicking and punching, and may even lead to death.
Emotional abuse
Emotional abuse includes sarcasm, degrading punishments, threats and not giving love and affection, which can undermine a young person's confidence.

Neglect

Neglect occurs when basic needs, such as food, warmth and medical care, are not met. Being thrown out of home may also be an example of neglect.

Sexual abuse

Sexual abuse occurs if an adult pressurises or forces a young person to take part in any kind of sexual activity. This can include kissing, touching the young person's genitals or breasts, intercourse or oral sex. If an adult asks you to touch his or her genitals, or to look at pornographic magazines or videos, these are also examples of sexual abuse.

As well as causing suffering at the time, there may be long-term difficulties for young people who have been abused. All forms of abuse are wrong and have damaging effects on children and young people.

Not getting you own way all the time is not an example of child abuse.

Why does it happen?

No one knows exactly why some adults take advantage of their position of authority over young people in this way. There may be many different reasons. Stress, money problems, unhappy circumstances, the feeling of having no power in adult relationships, and having been abused as a child may all play a part. But it is hard to predict with certainty which factors cause an adult to abuse a child.

Some adults may even convince themselves that there is nothing wrong with their behaviour, or that it is for the child's own good.

But whatever the reason, abuse is always wrong and it is never the young person's fault.

Is that a fact?

Try our quiz below. Cover the answers, and decide whether the statement is either true or false for each question. Check your answers and see how well you did.

1. When a young person is abused, the offender is usually a stranger.
True or false?

2. Young people are always taken into care if abuse is suspected.
True or false?

3. Abuse only happens in poor families.
True or false?

4. The NSPCC helps adults, as well as young people and children.
True or false?

5. Abusing very young children is not that bad, because the children won't remember much about it when they are grown up.
True or false?

Answers

1. *False*. The abuser is a total stranger in only one in every six or seven reported cases of abuse of young people and children.
2. *False*. Young people are taken away from their families in only a very small number of cases, when it is thought dangerous for them to stay at home. Most return home, just as soon as it is felt they will be safe.
3. *False*. Child abuse can happen in any kind of family.
4. *True*. The NSPCC gives counselling to adults who were abused as children, or who are in danger of abusing their own children.
5. *False*. People who are abused when they were very young may not remember exactly what happened to them, but they may well experience emotional and psychological problems during their teens and adult life.

All about the NSPCC

The NSPCC's job is to work to prevent child abuse and to protect children and young people from abuse and neglect.

We hear about young people and children at risk from concerned relatives, friends, neighbours, teachers, health or childcare professionals, and also children and young people themselves.

Staff from the NSPCC's teams and projects work with the whole family to stop abuse happening. They will help young people and children to understand that they are not to blame for the harm they have suffered, and to recover from their experiences. Child protection staff also encourage parents to take responsibility for their actions and to learn how to meet their children's needs.

The NSPCC often works closely with other organisations and people concerned with young people and children, including social workers, doctors and police officers.

Photo: Larry Bray / ChildLine. Posed by model.

Child protection

The issues – information from NCH Action for Children

The last year has been dominated by revelations about abuse of children in public care, and a number of tragic cases of children having been sexually abused and killed by sex offenders, leading to a public outcry over the release of such offenders into the community. In addition to these high profile issues, those involved professionally have been preoccupied by the need to respond to *Messages from Research, 1995* on the child protection system. This has now become known as the refocusing debate.

The Department of Health has called for 'children's services to focus on ensuring that child protection is firmly placed within a context of wider work to support children in need and their families'. The research shows that less than half of referrals are ever substantiated and that it is expensive. Therefore, many local authorities and voluntary organisations are reviewing their services. Consequently, innovative approaches, such as family group conferences and mediation in child protection are being piloted across the UK.

Paul Boateng, the new health minister with responsibility for children's services in England, has stated his wish to broaden the scope of the department's refocusing initiative beyond family support and child protection to embrace parenting as a whole. A major governmental thrust is towards the recognition that early intervention is not only most effective in enhancing people's lives and opportunities, but it is also cost effective.

In Scotland, the introduction of the Children (Scotland) Act 1995 is underpinned by a similar approach and is to be welcomed.

The National Commission of

Photo: Larry Bray / ChildLine. Posed by model

Inquiry into the prevention of child abuse published their report, *Childhood Matters*, in late 1996. The Inquiry took evidence from more than ten thousand people, including those who themselves had suffered abuse as a child. Although the Inquiry will continue to implement and disseminate its findings, some uncomfortable truths have already emerged. These include:

- At least half of the abuse that occurs, sometimes over lengthy periods of a child's life, remains undisclosed at the time of occurrence.
- Despite a series of wide-ranging and well-publicised expensive inquiries into instances of child abuse and neglect over twenty years, and despite the flow of recommendations they produced, the abuses persist largely unaffected by such efforts as have been taken to prevent them.

In June 1997, a joint campaign by Community Care and ChildLine, *Child Protection: everybody's business*, was launched. The report, an analysis of 7,215 calls by adults to ChildLine, with wide-ranging concerns about child protection, presents a number of messages. These include 'the pressing need for confidential help from professionals'. The overriding message was that the wider community needs greater awareness of the reality of child abuse and the professional response, and that the safeguarding of children is a community responsibility.

Child protection registers

Social Services Departments hold a central register of all children in their area considered to be at risk of abuse and for whom there is an inter-agency protection plan. Registration takes place as a result of a child protection conference, which makes decisions about the level of risk to the child and whether they should be placed on the register. If a child's name is placed on the register, the case conference will also draw up an inter-agency agreement to work co-operatively to protect the child. Registers do not reflect the true extent of child abuse for two main reasons. First, not every case of child abuse is reported and second many cases are resolved without the need to enter the child on the register. It is important to note that some children on the register will not have been victims of actual abuse, they may have been registered because it was considered that there was a likelihood that they would suffer abuse in the future.

Categories of abuse

The category of abuse under which a child is registered is a matter of professional judgement. This will normally have been made at the case conference, when it was agreed that registration was necessary. The definitions of abuse are as set out in the Department of Health's *Working Together under the Children Act 1989*, para. 6.40:

Neglect
The persistent or severe neglect of a child or the failure to protect a child from exposure to any kind of danger, including cold or starvation, or extreme failure to carry out important aspects of care, resulting in significant impairment of the child's health or development, including non-organic failure to thrive.

Physical abuse
Actual or likely physical injury to a child, or failure to prevent physical injury (or suffering) to a child, including deliberate poisoning, suffocation and Munchausen's syndrome by proxy.

Sexual abuse
Actual or likely sexual exploitation of a child or adolescent. The child may be dependent and/or developmentally immature.

Emotional abuse
Actual or likely severe adverse effect on the emotional and behavioural development of a child caused by persistent or severe emotional ill-treatment or rejection. All abuse involves some emotional ill-treatment. This category is used where it is the main or sole form of abuse.

Working Together does not include 'grave concern' as a category of abuse. It has not been available as a category for registration since 14 October 1991. Children who were previously categorised under 'grave concern' were to be re-categorised at their next case review. The definition of 'grave concern' used to be:

Children whose situations do not currently fit the above categories, but where social and medical assessment indicate that they are at significant risk of abuse. These could include situations where another child in the household has been harmed, or the household contains a known abuser.

Child protection registers in England

As of March 31st, 1996 there were 32,351 children on child protection registers. This represents 29 children per 10,000 population aged under 18, a decrease of 7 per cent in number and 9 per cent in rates compared to the numbers registered in 1995.

During the year ending 31st March 1996 there were a total of 28,270 registrations and 30,462 deregistrations. This represents a 7 per cent decrease in registrations and a one per cent increase in deregistrations compared to 1995.

The number of registrations, and numbers on the register for boys and girls, varies considerably by age and category of abuse. Younger children are more likely to be on the registers than older children, 8 per cent were aged one to four and 30 per cent five to nine.

Two out of five registrations related to those considered at risk of physical injury. A third were considered at risk of neglect and 22 per cent at risk of sexual abuse of which figure girls constituted 61 per cent. Of those registered under the category of physical injury, 54 per cent were boys. First registrations represented about 82% of all registrations. Of the 44,100 initial child protection conferences held during the year ending 31st March 1996, 28,270 (64%) led to registration.

In 1991 the number of children and young people on child protection registers reached a peak of just over 45,000. The numbers have since fallen to around 32,000 in 1996. In part, this fall has occurred because of new guidance abolishing the category of 'grave concern'.
Source: *Children and Young People on Child Protection Registers, year ending 31 March 1996, England.* Department of Health, 1997.

Child protection registers: England

	Registrations			On the register		
	1994	1995	1996	1994	1995	1996
All ages	28500	30444	28270	34900	34954	32351
Under 1	4000	4100	3800	2700	2900	2600
1 to 4	8300	8900	8100	10500	10800	9900
5 to 9	8000	8600	8000	10700	10600	10000
10 to 15	7500	7900	7200	9700	9600	8800
16+	500	600	600	1100	900	900
%						
Under 1	14	14	14	8	8	8
1 to 4	29	30	29	30	31	31
5 to 9	28	29	28	31	30	31
10 to 15	27	26	26	28	28	27
16+	2	2	2	3	3	3
Category						
Neglect	7800	9200	9400	10300	11200	11162
Physical injury	11400	12300	10700	13000	13000	11377
Sexual abuse	7500	7200	6200	9600	9200	7728
Emotional abuse	3500	3800	4000	4400	4700	4973
Other	500	400	800	500	300	716
%						
Neglect	27	30	33	30	32	35
Physical injury	40	40	38	37	37	35
Sexual abuse	26	24	22	28	26	24
Emotional abuse	12	13	14	13	13	15
Other	2	1	3	2	1	3

Source: *Children and Young People on Child Protection Registers, year ending 31 March 1996.* DoH 1997

Protecting children from abuse

A guide for everyone involved in children's sport

Child abuse is a very emotive and difficult subject – especially if you think your child or a child you know is being harmed. This information is written for everyone involved in children's sport. You may be a parent wanting to ensure your children are as safe as possible at the club; a teacher or helper worried about a child you coach or concerned about the behaviour of the club manager or coach; a sports development or National Governing Body (NGB) officer who is worried about the behaviour of the team manager or club secretary. This information explains what child abuse is, how to recognise it and what to do if you have concerns. It offers advice for parents, coaches and sports organisations to ensure they do everything they can to protect children from abuse.

What is child abuse?

Child abuse is a term used to describe ways in which children are harmed, usually by adults and often by people they know and trust. It refers to the damage done to a child's physical or mental health. Children can be abused within or outside their family, at school and even in the sports environment. Child abuse can take many forms:

Physical abuse, where adults:

- physically hurt or injure children (e.g. by hitting, shaking, squeezing, biting or burning)
- give children alcohol, inappropriate drugs or poison
- attempt to suffocate or drown children.

In sport situations, physical abuse might also occur when the nature and intensity of training exceeds the capacity of the child's immature and growing body.

Neglect

Neglect includes situations in which adults:

- fail to meet a child's basic physical needs (e.g. for food, warm clothing)
- consistently leave children alone and unsupervised
- fail or refuse to give children love, affection or attention.

Neglect in a sports situation might also occur if a teacher or coach fails to ensure children are safe or exposes them to undue cold or risk of injury.

Sexual abuse

Boys and girls are sexually abused when adults (male or female) use them to meet their own sexual needs. This could include:

- full sexual intercourse, masturbation, oral sex, fondling
- showing children pornographic books, photographs or videos, or taking pictures for pornographic purposes.

Sports situations which involve physical contact (e.g. supporting or guiding children) could potentially create situations where sexual abuse may go unnoticed. Abusive situations may also occur if adults misuse their power over young people.

Emotional abuse

Emotional abuse can occur in a number of ways. For example, where:

- there is a persistent lack of love or affection
- there is constant overprotection which prevents children from socialising
- children are frequently being shouted at or taunted
- there is neglect, physical or sexual abuse.

Emotional abuse in sport might also include situations where parents or coaches subject children to constant criticism, bullying or unrealistic pressure to perform to high expectations.

How would you recognise a child is being abused?

There are signs which could alert you to the fact that a child might be being abused. These would include:

- unexplained bruising or injuries
- sexually explicit language or actions
- sudden changes in behaviour
- something a child has said
- a change observed over a long period of time (e.g. the child losing weight or becoming increasingly dirty or unkempt).

However, it is important to note that a child could be displaying some or all of these signs, or behaving in a way which is worrying – this does not necessarily mean the child is being abused. Similarly, there may not be any signs, you may just feel something is wrong. If you are worried, it is not your responsibility to decide if it is abuse but it is your responsibility to act on your concerns and do something about it.

Social Services and the Police have a duty under the Children Act to ensure children are protected and to help those who have been abused. They are trained to deal with child abuse and should be contacted when there are concerns. They will give you advice and take responsibility for any action which is necessary.

What should I do if I have concerns?

1. If you have noticed a change in the child's behaviour, first talk to the parents or carers. It may be that something has happened, like a bereavement, which has caused the child to be unhappy. However, if your concerns are about sexual abuse or violence, talking to the parents or carers might put the child at greater risk.
2. If your concerns remain or you cannot talk to the parents/carers, consult the person in charge or someone you can trust. It is the responsibility of the person in charge to make the decision to contact Social Services.
3. If the person in charge is not available, or the concerns are about him/her, or you do not feel appropriate action has been taken, you must contact Social Services or the Police yourself. The number is in the phone book. If you want to talk things through to gain some advice, you can phone the NSPCC free HelpLine: 0800 800 500. This operates 24 hours a day, every day. You do not have to give your name but it is helpful if you can.

What will happen next?

Social Services have a responsibility to investigate all concerns about child abuse. They do this jointly with the Police. This may involve talking to the child and his/her family and/or gathering more information. If allegations have been made against a coach or member of staff, this may involve suspension or disciplinary proceedings. If a crime has been committed, criminal investigations will take place.

What should I do if a child tells me s/he is being abused?

Always:

- stay calm – ensure the child is safe and feels safe
- show and tell the child that you are taking what s/he says seriously
- reassure the child and stress that s/he is not to blame
- be honest, explain you will have to tell someone else to help stop the abuse
- make a note of what the child has said as soon as possible after the event
- maintain confidentiality – only tell others if it will help protect the child.

Never:

- rush into actions that may be inappropriate
- make promises you cannot keep
- take sole responsibility – consult someone else (the person in charge or someone you can trust) so you can begin to protect the child and gain support for yourself.

If I do something, might it make things worse?

Taking appropriate action if you are worried about abuse is never easy – it takes courage but it protects a young life. You may be upset about what the child has said or you may worry about the consequences of your actions. Sometimes people worry about children being removed from their families as a result of abuse but in reality this rarely happens. However, one thing is certain – you cannot ignore it. The effects of abuse on children can be devastating, especially if children are left unprotected or do not receive help to cope with the abuse. The most serious effect is that children can and do die as a result of abuse. They can develop behavioural difficulties, problems at school, their development can be delayed and they can become depressed and withdrawn. Some of these problems, if left untreated, can persist into adulthood.

What can I do to protect my child or children in my sport from abuse?

If you are a parent or carer:

- check to see if the club has a policy which ensures children are protected and kept safe from harm
- check that staff and volunteers are carefully recruited, trained and supervised
- know how to voice your concerns or complain if there is anything you are not happy about
- ensure your children know how to voice their concerns or complain if there is anything they are not happy about
- encourage your child to talk to you about any worries.

If you are a coach/member of staff/volunteer:

You can reduce situations for abuse of children and help to protect staff and volunteers by promoting good practice. Everyone should be aware that, as a general rule, it does not make sense to:

- spend excessive amounts of time alone with children away from others
- take children alone in a car on journeys, however short
- take children to your home.

Where any of these are unavoidable, ensure they only occur with the full knowledge and consent of someone in charge in the organisation or the child's parents.

You should never:

- engage in rough, physical or sexually provocative games, including horseplay
- allow or engage in inappropriate touching of any form
- allow children to use inappropriate language unchallenged
- make sexually suggestive comments to a child, even in fun
- let allegations a child makes go unchallenged or unrecorded. Always act.
- do things of a personal nature that children can do for themselves. However, it may be sometimes necessary for your staff or volunteers to do things of a personal nature for children, particularly if they are very young or disabled. These tasks should only be carried out with the full understanding and consent of parents. In an emergency situation which requires this type of help, parents should be fully informed.

In such situations, it is important to ensure all staff are sensitive to the child and undertake personal care tasks with the utmost discretion.

Where can I get further help?

Useful 24-hour free telephone numbers for advice or further help:
ChildLine: 0800 1111
NSPCC HelpLine: 0800 800 500

Out alone

Keeping children safe when out with you or out alone

Are your children safe?

This article gives practical advice on keeping children safe outside the home. It also encourages you to think about ways of making the world a safer place for children. Acting to stop them being hurt, or complaining about unsafe roads or playgrounds may not always be easy, but unless we are prepared to, things will never change.

Most high streets weren't designed for families with young children. Many things can make it difficult to keep them safe – feeling stressed, too many cars, crowded buses, and shops that don't welcome children or pushchairs.

It is difficult to set an exact age when it's safe for children to be out alone. Around the age of eight or nine they may want to be more independent and be out with friends, but you must first make absolutely sure they can cope and have developed road sense. Children who are less mature, or those with a disability, may not be safe out alone until they're much older.

With older children, the problems are just as worrying. How can you protect them from harm, yet allow them enough freedom to become confident and independent?

Getting the balance right isn't always easy, but there is a lot parents can do to prepare children for being out on their own.

How can you stop toddlers from wandering off in a shopping centre? What should you tell children to do if they get lost? When are they old enough to go out on their own? And what should you do if you see a distressed child?

Read on for some practical tips and advice . . .

Remember, it is adults who are responsible for the safety and well-being of children.

What's your verdict?

Three families tell us their stories. When you've read each one, say whether you think the parents' actions were OK or not OK. Then compare your answers with the advice.

1. 'I pick up Joe from nursery after work, and then do the shopping on my way home. It's a rush to fetch my daughter from school by half three. Joe always whines to get out of the buggy, but it slows me down too much. I leave him in the buggy outside the shop – there's usually someone around to keep an eye on him. Otherwise I often end up smacking him to make him sit still.'

2. Maria is seven and Paul is five. It's not much fun for them stuck indoors, so I sometimes let them go to the shops for me on their own, or to the playground until dinner is ready. It stops them getting under my feet, and it's probably good for them.

3. 'Now that Lizzy is eight we let her walk to school and back on her own. It's only about 10 minutes away and she knows to be careful crossing the main road. We both work full time, so we don't have much choice.'

Now let's look at it from the children's point of view . . .

1a. It is never safe to leave a young child alone in a public place. The risk may be small, but it would only take a minute for him to be abducted. And never ask people you don't know to 'keep an eye' on him. However well-meaning they may seem, you can't know that they can be trusted. Remember too that children don't understand adult pressures or timing. Slapping or shouting will only make your child more upset and his behaviour worse. Why not include him as much as you can in the shopping, by letting him put things in the basket, for example? Reins or a safety harness could give him a safe break from the buggy. If

Photo: Duncan Ridgley / NSPCC. Posed by models

nothing seems to work, think about shopping later in the evening when a partner or friend may be able to babysit.

2a. All children need fresh air, exercise and the chance to be independent, but in most situations it is not safe to allow children this young to be completely out of sight, or to be sent shopping alone. What if they were hurt at the playground and unable to call for help, or they tried to cross a busy road and got run over? Some children may get worried or have arguments that they can't sort out on their own. There is also the small possibility that they might be bullied by older children or approached by an adult who could harm them. If possible, let them play where you can see them from the window, or try to go to the park with them sometimes. They will enjoy having you there and you will know that they are safe.

3a. Children this young are rarely able to judge the speed of cars, so it is not safe for them to be alone near busy roads. Apart from this and many other safety risks, your child may feel 'different' from friends who aren't left alone in the playground and who are picked up by someone they can talk to about the day's events. Is there another parent who could share the school trips with you, or who might do it in return for some babysitting? The school may know of someone. Or get together with other parents and ask the school to organise an 'after school club' or 'early bird' scheme, where parents can drop children off before they go to work.

Remember, try to be aware of children's needs and their understanding of time, and don't always expect them to fit in with yours.

10 ways to keep children safe

1. In most situations, children under about eight years old shouldn't be out alone, especially in busy towns. Even when out playing with other children, they need to be kept in the care and sight of an adult or a much older child who is mature and trustworthy.
2. Never leave young children in unsupervised play areas in shops or parks. And don't leave them alone in the car or outside a shop, not even for a few minutes.
3. If you're in a crowded place, keep children in a pram or buggy, hold hands tightly, or use reins. Don't walk far ahead of small children who can't keep up. Remember, it only takes a moment for toddlers to wander off.
4. As soon as children are able to understand, teach them their full name, address and telephone number. Practise these with them until you're sure they can remember.
5. You can start teaching children simple rules about personal safety from as young as two or three. Tell them clearly that they must never go off with anyone, not even someone they know, without first asking you or the adult who is looking after them. Turn it into a game you can play when you pick them up from nursery.
6. Teach older children safe ways of crossing roads, going shopping and asking adults for directions, and let them practise these with you until you are sure that they have understood. When they are mature enough to be out alone, make sure they tell you: Who they're going out with. Where they're going (if possible get a phone number where you can reach them). When they will be back.
7. In busy public places, arrange somewhere safe to meet in case you get separated, like an information desk or cash point. Make sure that children know what to do if they ever get lost, and who is safest to ask for help – a police officer, shop assistant or someone with a young child.
8. Help to build your child's self-esteem with lots of love, praise and attention. Bullies and dangerous adults may tend to pick out less confident children or those who are neglected and often left alone.
9. Let children know that they never have to do anything they don't like with an adult or older child – even if it's someone they know. Practise this at home by never making them kiss or hug an adult if they don't want to.
10. Listen to your children, especially when they are trying to tell you about things that worry them. Is there a bully at school or a babysitter they don't like? Let children know that you will always take them seriously and do whatever you can to keep them safe.

When to take action

Keeping children safe is everybody's business. It can be difficult to know when to act and what to do, especially when another adult is involved. You may feel embarrassed or afraid of the adult's reaction. And you certainly don't want to make things worse for the child. The important thing is to try and stop children being hurt. It's better to seem like a busybody than to ignore a child who may be in danger.

If you see a distressed child that you think is being bullied, stop and ask why the child is upset. Get help from other adults passing by if you need to. If you're still concerned, get a good description of those involved and phone the police. Don't give up until you're sure the child is safe.

It can be even harder to take action if you see a child being ill-treated by an adult. Sadly, many people accept this or think that it isn't their business. Unless we are brave enough to act, attitudes will never change and children will continue to be hurt. Offer to help. If you try to be kind and positive, you will be doing the right thing. If your offer of help is refused but you are really worried about the child's safety, get a good description and ring the police.

If you aren't able to help a family you know who may be in trouble, or if you know of a child who may be in danger, please ring the local police, social services or the NSPCC Child Protection Helpline at once. The NSPCC takes action to protect children. We will listen, advise and respond to what you say.

NSPCC child protection helpline: 0800 800 500.

No matter how much you teach your child about safety, remember the limits of their age and maturity.

• The above is an extract from *Out alone – Keeping children safe when out with you or out alone*, produced by the NSPCC. See page 41 for address details.

International conference says even a cuff should be outlawed

It's been a bad day, the children have been hell, then they really start misbehaving. Are you right to smack them? By Jojo Moyes

Campaigners from 25 countries yesterday called for a change in the law to make the smacking of children as unacceptable as wife beating.

The International Conference on the Ending of Physical Punishment of Children in Dublin wants slapping children to be made illegal by 2000.

'The basic target is to change attitudes and make it quite clear that it is no more acceptable to hit a child than it is to hit your friends or your wife, or anyone else,' conference coordinator, Peter Newall, said.

But he stressed that the purpose of a law making smacking of children illegal was 'wholly educational' and aimed at changing attitudes rather than putting parents in the dock.

He told BBC Radio 4 that this did not mean punishing more parents. 'There are now six or possibly seven countries in Europe that have taken this step . . . The result has not been any increase in prosecutions of parents. Far from it. By changing attitudes towards children it actually reduces the need for formal interventions.'

The issue of smacking is a contentious one. Earlier this year the Prime Minister, Tony Blair, reignited the debate when he admitted he had occasionally taken a hand to his children.

'I always regretted it because there are lots of ways of disciplining a child, and I don't believe that belting them is the best one,' Mr Blair said at the time. But he added: 'There is a clear dividing line between administering discipline on the one hand and violence on the other, which most parents understand perfectly well.'

Last November, leading childcare experts and lawyers called for a national strategy to tackle violence by and against children, including a smacking ban.

The Commission on Children and Violence, which was set up in the wake of the murder of James Bulger in 1993 by two 11-year-old boys, concluded that violent tendencies begin in childhood. It found that one in six children still experiences violent punishment and many are beaten with belts and canes.

The commission, which heard from 400 organisations and 500 children, said such 'negative, violent and humiliating forms of discipline' should be banned, as these become 'significant in the development of violent attitudes and actions from a very early age'.

This was reiterated yesterday by the charity Childline, which said that it recommended other ways, such as the implementation of sanctions, to discourage bad behaviour.

'We don't think smacking is a good idea. What we find from what children tell us is that parents . . . when they're under stress, can find themselves becoming rather more violent,' a spokeswoman, Wendy Toms, said. 'We hear terrible, terrible incidents described to us by children of smacking that escalates.'

She said the charity was not joining the call for smacking to be made illegal, which it did not believe was practicable. 'But we do think there should be a ban on people other than parents smacking children – it's not appropriate for others, such as childminders,' she added.

Crimes and punishment

It's the dilemma facing all parents: how to discipline your child without smacking. Maureen Freely looks at the alternatives

In Exeter last week, a judge put a 37-year-old stepfather on probation after hearing that he had forced his 13-year-old stepson to stand naked in the street wearing a sign that said, 'I am lazy and wet my bed'. The man also admitted to threatening behaviour, child cruelty and two assaults resulting in injury. A condition of his sentence is that he take a course to learn how to be a caring parent. But what exactly does that mean these days and does punishment play any part at all?

The nice middle-class liberal view is: the less punishment, the better. If you go overboard and hit or humiliate a child, then you've lost your moral authority. Your children may fear you for your unpredictable temper, but you will never have their respect. And that's what authority should depend on – not rods, canes, straps and dunce caps. This is not just a theory for those of us who have childhood memories of such devices, it's a legacy we're not keen to pass on.

But in our efforts to avoid sadistic extremes, we often end up avoiding punishment altogether. The best current thinking does not advise this head-in-the-sand approach: instead it looks to create a situation in which punishment is less necessary. It advises going back to the drawing board to redesign your daily routine so that there is little opportunity for bad behaviour and lots of attention given to its desirable opposite. It encourages talk about the importance of good behaviour and agreement about goals.

Children should know exactly what the consequences will be if they break the contract. When they do break it, it is important that they see these consequences meted out fast and consistently. I know this sort of behaviour policy works because I've seen it in action in my daughter's school. But something has got lost in translation whenever I've tried it out in the discomfort of my own home.

I did have one great victory years ago, when my eldest son was 10. He had taken to having violent fits of temper. Afterwards he would tell me that he just couldn't help it because this was just the way boys were. Instead of trying to talk him out of his convenient cultural prejudices, I made a chart and said that if he could go through a month without one tantrum I would buy him an expensive toy he'd been pining for. When he had made it through the month without a hitch, I was able to turn to him and point out that, actually, he could control his temper if he wanted to. And the tantrums stopped.

I was ready at that point to turn all life into a wall chart. But then I made friends with some people who had gone one step further, to create what you might call a behavioural version of a building society. Their children all received weekly allowances which they could increase with good deeds or decrease with bad ones. A graph on the refrigerator door kept track of their fluctuating accounts. It was always up to date, too – these parents never forgot to adjust the balance every morning, right after breakfast.

When I tried it in our house, I would forget to update the accounts for days at a time. This did not win me any respect from my increasingly irate customers and I got into more trouble – and lost lots of moral authority – by sometimes forgetting to enter a child's bad deed. There were lots of disputes about the value I put on various good and bad acts, and much resentment when they clocked up more good behaviour than my very tight budget permitted.

Most depressing was the amount of time I spent arguing with the children about money. This rather undercut my other lectures about the money being unimportant. So after a few weeks I gave up on punishment prevention schemes and went back to my old non-violent standbys.

But I've never found these really worked either. You can't get a toddler to stop running into the road, for example, by appealing to his reason. And the other mild forms of deprivation and exclusion seem an inadequate response to bad behaviour. Imagine trying to scare a really naughty child back into the strait-jacket of civilisation by saying, 'If you keep this up, you know, there's no more ice cream,' or 'I've had it. Go to your room.'

My own first offering is even more pathetic: 'If you don't watch out, I'm going to get angry.' The problem is, I put so much effort into avoiding escalation that I really am angry by the time I have removed a kicking screaming bundle to her bedroom. I look and sound like a monster even if, technically speaking, I don't act like one. I'm sure this causes a deeper and more lasting scar than a spanking would have done. If nothing else, I'm impressing on this child the idea that she has to obey me, because I am more powerful than she is.

But of course, that is the same message she will have got from all those lost ice creams and forced trips to the bedroom. It is not a message any egalitarian child ever accepts –

If you go overboard and hit or humiliate a child, then you've lost your moral authority

and why should she, if all she stands to lose is a scoop of ice cream? It doesn't take long, anyway, before they are old enough to work out that the ice cream punishment falls apart the moment they say they don't like ice cream anyway, and that slamming five doors en route to the bedroom is a good way of getting even while upping the ante.

Even in households where parents are struggling not to be sadists, the punishments get cleverer and more devious as children get older and bolshier. Parents do not give up the fight just because they're no longer strong enough to carry their children to their rooms or block their access to the freezer. Instead we withhold adult privileges like money and freedom, we stun with sarcasm and force teenagers into submission by waging psychological terrorism that leaves no marks.

You want examples? Well, I got a lot of mileage a few years ago out of some embarrassing baby pictures, and when that stopped working all I had to do was threaten to show up in front of eldest daughter's school wearing a dress she thought was too young for me.

It's exhausting, all this game-playing. And, because the person with the most experience always has the advantage, it feels dishonest. If you're like me and uncomfortable about playing the voice of authority in the first place – because it seems hypocritical, disrespectful or undemocratic – it is easy to forget that there's more to authority than keeping the upper hand and that part of your job as a parent is to prepare your children to deal with other, less benign authorities.

Fair and thoughtful punishments can equip a child for the school of life far better than blanket niceness ever will. The cruellest thing you can do to any child is send him or her out into the world without having first taught them that bad behaviour has consequences.

Great and good support Carey over smacking

By Flora Hunter and Catherine Elsworth

The Archbishop of Canterbury won wide support yesterday for his defence of the 'gentle slap' as a way of teaching children right from wrong.

Dr George Carey was criticised by children's charities, but politicians and Church leaders said he was reflecting the views of ordinary parents. Supporters welcomed what they called his 'commonsense' approach to discipline, which advocates a gentle slap 'as long as it is done with love and firm discipline within the family'.

Lord Tebbit, a former chairman of the Conservative Party, described the advice as eminently sensible. 'I

'We are not talking about beating them up, but a little slap doesn't do them any harm. The key thing is that it brings you up sharp'

was caned at school and I suspect that I would have been more unruly had I not been,' he said. 'As far as disciplining our children went, we followed the archbishop's advice.'

David Clark, the shadow defence secretary, said there were very few families where children had not been given the 'odd slap'. He said: 'We are not talking about beating them up, but a little slap doesn't do them any harm. The key thing is that it brings you up sharp.'

His front-bench colleague, David Blunkett, Labour's Education

Minister, agreed: 'There are very few children in the world who have never, ever been smacked. If it is a last resort and used only in very unusual circumstances, then I think it is a perfectly reasonable way of bringing home the severity of what a child has done.'

Mr Blunkett said it was important to distinguish between smacking and physical violence.

Sir Ivan Lawrence, Conservative MP for Burton, said the archbishop's comments were in 'total accordance with common sense and the experience of most parents. I got a good hiding at home and at school if I was bad. It didn't do me any harm; in fact, I like to think it probably did me some good.'

The Rt Rev Noël Debroy Jones, Bishop of Sodor and Man, said: 'I feel the archbishop is saying things that every normal parent would say. I don't think the Church should be afraid to speak out on difficult subjects. There are places where discipline is necessary and, within a loving relationship, chastening, correction or discipline is a valid proposition.'

Anne Atkins, who caused a stir last month by criticising the Church of England's attitude to morality on the *Today* programme's 'Thought for the Day', said she thought few intelligent people would disagree with Dr Carey. 'Children do need disciplining, and I would agree with his point that it should be done within the context of love.' She said the matter was not particularly controversial. 'It would be lovely to have a moral lead from the archbishop on more controversial issues.'

Dr Carey's entry to the contentious debate on corporal punishment has inevitably angered some.

Sir William Utting, who chaired a commission on children and violence last year, said that it was dangerous to condone even gentle slapping, because it could send out the wrong message.

'Obviously if a parent taps a child gently, in the context of a loving relationship, to teach them right from wrong, it probably won't damage that child,' he said. 'However, by supporting that, one is in danger of supporting a culture in which people use disproportionate violence.'

Joan Bakewell, the broadcaster whose series, *Heart of the Matter*, debates moral issues, said: 'Smacking is an admission that you have failed as a parent to find another way of disciplining your child.

'I was smacked as a child and it just made me stubborn.'

Have you hit your children?

Michael Howard, Stephen Dorrell and Tony Blair, have all publicly admitted slapping their children. The Sunday Telegraph asked a range of high-profile parents whether they had ever used corporal punishment.

Norman Tebbit, the former Conservative Party chairman: was caned as a child and favours firm discipline. Confirmed that he and his wife had 'followed the archbishop's advice'.

Joan Bakewell, the broadcaster: believes parents should avoid smacking in favour of other forms of discipline.

Sir William Utting, former Chief Inspector of Social Services: chaired a commission on children and violence last year which came out firmly against any physical form of parental discipline, however mild. Admitted he had slapped his own children.

Anne Atkins, the novelist and Thought for the Day contributor: believes a gentle slap is acceptable within a loving home environment.

Beryl Bainbridge, the novelist: thinks that it is wrong to smack children and that it will not teach them right from wrong.

David Clark, the Defence Secretary: says a gentle slap in the right circumstances can't do any harm. Admitted that he had slapped his own children.

The Rt Rev Colin Buchanan, bishop designate of Woolwich: supports the archbishop's view but says there must be limits. Did not slap his children.

Sir Ivan Lawrence, the Conservative MP: insists there is nothing wrong with 'a good hiding', but refused to say whether he had smacked his daughter, who is now 28.

Hitting children

An international habit

'Corporal punishment is so widespread that it is part of growing up for most children in most countries of the world'.

Murray A Straus, *Beating the devil out of them*, Lexington Books, 1994.

'The majority of British parents we have interviewed seem to believe that physical punishment is an effective and probably necessary aspect of ordinary child upbringing'.

John and Elizabeth Newson, child psychologists.

In South Africa until 1993, up to 30,000 young offenders were whipped each year. But in 1995 the Constitutional Court of the new South Africa declared whipping unconstitutional, and the Government has announced that physical punishment will be pro-hibited in the school and child care systems.

In August 1987, the UK became the last country in Western Europe to end school corporal punishment in all states supported education (it is still allowed in some private schools). In the USA, only 27 of the 50 states had banned corporal punishment in public schools by 1996.

Where physical punishment of children has been recognised as an issue deserving attention, research into attitudes and prevalence has generally found a large majority of parents hitting children frequently, from a very early age, with hands, sticks, belts and other implements.

In the United Kingdom a large government-sponsored survey whose first results were published in 1995 found that almost one in six children had experienced 'severe' physical punishment; the large majority (91 per cent) had been hit, 77 per cent in the last year. More than a third of four-year-olds were hit more than once a week; three-quarters of one-year-old babies had been hit in the year preceding the interviews.

In the USA, a 1985 survey of a representative sample of 3,232 families with children under 17 found that 89 per cent of parents had hit their three-year-old child during the previous year; about a third of 15- to 17-year-olds had been hit.

In Barbados in the West Indies, a 1987 survey found 70 per cent of respondents 'generally approving' of parental physical punishment; of these 76 per cent endorsed beating children with belts or straps.

In Australia, a 1987 study of primary school children revealed that 81 per cent of boys and 74 per cent of girls had been hit by their mother, 76 per cent of boys and 63 per cent of girls by their father.

In Korea, a 1982 survey by the Child Protection Association found 97 per cent of interviewed children had been physically punished, many severely.

Physical punishment is a 'common disciplinary practice' in India: a survey of university students, reported in 1991, found 91 per cent of males and 86 per cent of females had been physically punished in their childhood.

Results of a detailed study in Chile, published in 1995, involved interviewing a large sample of parents and children from two state schools, and smaller samples from a private fee-paying Catholic school. Child 'battering' was admitted by 80.4 per cent (state schools) and 56.7 per cent (private school).

In Romania, a survey in 1992 found that 84 per cent of a sample of parents regarded spanking as a normal method of childrearing. 96 per cent did not consider it humiliating.

In Europe: pressure for reform

Within Europe by 1996 six countries had prohibited all physical punishment of children, and the Council of Europe has encouraged its 33 member-states to follow suit.

In 1985, proposing measures to reduce family violence the Committee of Ministers of the Council recommended that states should 'review their legislation on the power to punish children in order to limit or indeed prohibit corporal punishment even if violation of such a prohibition does not necessarily entail a criminal penalty' (R85/4).

In 1990 a further recommendation, on social measures concerning violence in the family, emphasised 'the general condemnation of corporal punishment and other forms of degrading treatment as a means of education and the need for violence-free education'.

And a 1993 recommendation on the 'medico-social aspects of child abuse' urged states to 'minimise levels of violence within society and the resort to violence in child-rearing practices'.

European Convention on Human Rights

In 1978 the European Court of Human Rights in Strasbourg ruled that judicial birching of a juvenile breached Article 3 of the European Convention, which bars 'inhuman or degrading treatment or punishment' (Tyrer v UK). Commission decisions on applications made by UK school children and their parents on school corporal punishment led to abolition in all state-supported education in the UK in 1987. In 1993 the Court found that punishment of a boy in a UK private school (he had been whacked three times with a soft-soled shoe on his clothed buttocks) did not breach the Convention; but the judgment was by five votes to four, and the Court emphasised that it did not approve in any way of school corporal punishment, and that the treatment was at or near the borderline.

In another significant case in 1982, the European Human Rights Commission rejected an application by Swedish parents alleging that Sweden's ban on parental physical punishment breached their right to respect for family life. The Commission concluded: 'The actual effects of the law are to encourage a positive review of the punishment of children by their parents, to discourage abuse and to prevent excesses which could properly be described as violence against children'.

'It is the very assumption that corporal punishment of children is legitimate that opens the way to all kinds of excesses and makes the traces of symptoms of such punishment acceptable to third parties.'

Council of Europe Committee of Ministers Recommendation, Explanatory Memorandum.

'All children have the right to freedom from corporal punishment at school, from the police and in prisons and at home . . .'.

Children's Charter of South Africa, adopted by a representative group of children at the Children's Summit, Cape Town, June 1 1992.

'The time has come to break bad habits which tend to be passed from one generation to the next. Legal and other affirmative action should be taken against all physical punishment and deliberate humiliation of children. Their rights apply as much within the family as outside.'

Concluding statement by General Rapporteur at Council of Europe conference on 'Evolution of the role of children in family life', Madrid, December 1994.

'By the prohibition of physical punishment, the legislator wanted to show that a child is an independent individual who can command full respect for his or her person, and who should thus have the same protection against physical punishment or violence as we adults see as being totally natural for ourselves.'

Swedish Ministry of Justice official explaining new law, 1979.

Banning physical punishment – a progress report

Progress towards protecting all the world's children from routine violence in their homes and in institutions is accelerating fast as we approach the new millennium. Recognition of children's rights under the UN Convention, and of the prevalence and dangers of physical punishment combine to add momentum to reforms which are now inevitable, but long overdue. In many countries physical punishment of children and young people has been prohibited in the penal system and in schools. And by 1996 six countries had banned ALL physical punishment of children – by parents and other carers as well as in institutions.

Sweden started a new epoch for children in 1979. Its family law was amended to read: 'Children are entitled to care, security and a good upbringing. Children are to be treated with respect for their person and individuality and may not be subjected to corporal punishment or any other humiliating treatment'.

Finland soon followed: its 1983 Child Custody and Rights of Access Act stated: 'A child shall be brought up in a spirit of understanding, security and love. He shall not be subdued, corporally punished or otherwise humiliated . . .'.

Since then four other countries – Denmark, Norway, Austria and Cyprus – have prohibited all physical punishment.

The purpose and effect of these laws has been to change attitudes to children and reduce violence, not to increase prosecution of parents, or state intervention in families. In Sweden, only one parent has been prosecuted in 12 years for 'ordinary' physical punishment. A father was given a small fine for spanking his 11-year-old son. But opinion polls have shown a dramatic change in attitudes to hitting children. By 1994, only 11 per cent of respondents to an opinion poll of Swedish adults 'approved of' physical punishment, compared with 65 per cent a few decades ago. And just one per cent of a large sample of Swedish 15-year-olds reported having been hit with an implement (compared with up to 25 per cent of children in some age groups in the UK and other countries which have resisted legal reform).

A major assessment of the effects of the Swedish law, carried out in 1981 and 1988, found: 'The law has dramatically reduced physical punishment and commitment to it. It has broken the inter-generational transmission of the practice. It has helped to reduce serious child-battering . . . Professionals in particular have welcomed having a "clear line" to transmit to parents'.

In Germany a draft Bill to end physical punishment is under consideration, strongly supported by the governmental Kinder Kommission and the West German Governmental Commission on 'Prevention and Control of Violence' (1990).

In Switzerland a governmental Commission on child abuse has proposed constitutional reform to uphold fully children's right to physical integrity. In Poland, a committee on constitutional reform has proposed a similar reform. In Spain proposed changes to family law forbid any level of violence to children. Government representatives from Croatia told the UN Committee in January 1996 that legislation banning physical punishment would be introduced shortly.

In 1994 the governmental Law Reform Commission in Ireland proposed that full prohibition of physical punishment should follow a government-sponsored education campaign.

In Canada, a federal Bill to remove the statutory confirmation of parents' and teachers' right to use physical punishment has been debated in Parliament, and the Departments of Justice and Health have promoted research and education campaigns on positive discipline.

In New Zealand, the Commissioner for Children (an independent office with statutory powers) has supported legal reform and launched an education campaign with booklets, posters, teaching packs and a book for children.

The 'right of correction' article has been removed from the Civil Code of the Federal District of Mexico City. But the article which gives parents the right to administer light blows to their children 'provided that they are not likely to endanger life and do not take longer than a fortnight to heal' is still included in the civil codes of the other 30 Mexican states.

In Namibia in 1991 the Supreme Court declared corporal punishment in government schools and the penal system to be unconstitutional, and the Ministry of Education launched an education campaign targeted at schools, communities and parents.

The Constitutional Court of the new South Africa declared penal whipping of young offenders to be unconstitutional in 1995, and the Government of National Unity announced that it would prohibit corporal punishment in all schools and welfare institutions.

There are active EPOCH-style campaigns in a number of countries, including Australia, Canada, South Africa and the US and over 60 organisations in countries in all continents have joined EPOCH WORLDWIDE, sharing the aim of ending all physical punishment through education and legal reform.

Parents' right to smack defended

By Patricia Wynn Davies, Legal affairs editor

Parents should keep the right to administer 'reasonable chastisement' of their children, the Government will argue before the European Commission of Human Rights on Monday. United Kingdom law should remain unchanged, it will argue, despite a series of court rulings that have sanctioned severe beatings, often involving the use of implements.

An application to the Commission in Strasbourg is being brought after a man was acquitted of assaulting his stepson. The boy, now 11, and his natural father are complaining that the punishment amounted to inhuman and degrading treatment, which is outlawed by article 3 of the European Convention on Human Rights, and that the state failed to secure protection of the boy's rights under the provision. He had been repeatedly caned between the ages of five and eight.

More than 60 children's and health organisations, including the National Children's Bureau, the National Society for the Prevention of Cruelty to Children, the British Paediatric Association and the National Childminding Association, have called for smacking, and all forms of physical punishment of children, to be outlawed.

In the case that emerged this week, a father was arrested and charged with slapping his 12-year-old son and was later bound over to keep the peace.

But far from outlawing smacking, UK law has proved it is prepared to countenance far more severe punishments. The 1933 Children and Young Persons Act allows parents and other carers to administer corporal punishment, leaving it to the courts to decide what amounts to 'reasonable' chastisement. In a series of cases, parents who beat their children with canes, electric flex, belts, whips and riding crops have been acquitted of assault or cruelty charges. Examples include a father who admitted taking down his teenage son's trousers and repeatedly hitting him with a belt, breaking his skin and causing bruising. He was acquitted by Cambridge magistrates.

The Government will argue that the 1933 law should remain in force and that the boy and his father have failed to exhaust UK legal remedies by failing to take out a civil action for assault against the stepfather.

If the application is declared 'admissible' it is likely to be referred for a full hearing by the European Court of Human Rights. If found to have breached the convention, the Government would be obliged, eventually, to change the law.

A smack today, but tearaway tomorrow

Smacking makes children violent and anti-social when they grow older, according to the latest US research.

The more often they are smacked, say experts, the more likely they are to cheat, lie, be disobedient and bully others.

Ending corporal punishment would lead to a reduction in anti-social behaviour in society, researchers believe.

British experts were sceptical about the claims, however.

They warned that the study could be flawed because it failed to recognise that children who were already badly behaved were most likely to be smacked.

Nine out of ten British parents – including Prime Minister Tony Blair – are prepared to admit they occasionally smack their children.

The study concludes that children who are smacked – even just once a week – show an increase in bad behaviour two years later.

More smacks lead to a higher level of misbehaviour, it claims.

Researchers at the University of New Hampshire studied 807 mothers who had at least one child aged between six and nine.

Ten per cent of mothers smacked their children three or more times a week, 14 per cent hit them twice and 20 per cent smacked their children once.

The study concludes that children who are smacked – even just once a week – show an increase in bad behaviour two years later

Researchers asked the mothers about their children's anti-social behaviour, which was scored on a system measuring whether the child cheated, told lies, bullied others, broke things deliberately and was disobedient at school.

The study, published yesterday in the Archives of Paediatrics and Adolescent Medicine, said the link between the amount of smacking and an increase in bad behaviour two years later was not affected by parenting style, class, the child's sex or ethnic background.

Dr Murray Straus, who led the researchers, said: 'Considering previous research showing that anti-social behaviour in childhood is associated with violence and other crime as an adult, society as a whole, not just children, could benefit from ending the system of violent child rearing that goes under the euphemism of spanking.'

The study said corporal punishment would aggravate behavioural problems rather than improving them.

Dr Straus added: 'Many people, probably most people, believe that if spanking is done by warm and loving parents, it has no harmful side effects, because kids know it's for their own good. That turns out not to be true.'

The study will contribute to the case made by more than 60 organisations, including the National Society for the Prevention of Cruelty to Children, for smacking and all forms of physical punishment to be outlawed.

And a spokesman for the anti-smacking group Epoch said the research was further proof that hitting children did not improve their behaviour.

Protect children from paedophiles

Advice and information for parents

Protect children

Parents who contact KIDSCAPE are worried about the best way to protect children, especially when they are out on their own. This article gives practical advice for keeping children safe and information on how paedophiles (people who sexually abuse children) target children.

Who are paedophiles?

- Paedophiles may seem perfectly respectable and 'nice'. They are extremely cunning and clever at worming their way into your confidence so that you trust them alone with your children.
- Paedophiles do not necessarily look dirty, weird or creepy or act suspiciously – they often behave like everyone else and look 'normal'.
- Paedophiles come from all classes, professions, racial and religious backgrounds.
- The majority of known paedophiles are male, though some women abuse children.
- 66% of paedophiles are known to the child, 34% are strangers.*

What paedophiles say

This information comes from the paedophiles themselves, who told KIDSCAPE how they ensnare children.*

- Paedophiles are good at making friends with children. They offer to teach them games, sports or how to play a musical instrument. They take them on outings, give them gifts, bribes, toys, money or treats and trick children into trusting them.
- Paedophiles often target single-parent families where mothers might be especially grateful for help with looking after the children.
- 48% of the paedophiles found their victims through babysitting.
- 30% of the paedophiles had each committed offences against 10 to 450 victims, 70% had between 1 to 10 victims.
- Paedophiles find victims by hanging round places children are likely to go, such as:
- arcades
- school premises
- shopping centres
- amusement or theme parks
- playgrounds
- parks
- swimming baths
- fairs
- fast food chains
- Be suspicious if someone is more interested in your children than in you, someone who always wants to babysit, take your children on outings – someone who wants to get your children alone.

What parents can do

- Check on anyone who is left in charge of your children or wants to spend time alone with them, especially babysitters. Talk (not just write) to other people they have worked for.
- Encourage discussions about personal safety, getting lost, and bullying by playing 'What if?' games with children.
- Practise the KIDSCAPE rule 'Yell, Run, Tell' with children so they feel confident about using safety strategies.
- Explain to children the difference between 'safe' and 'unsafe' secrets. A secret about a surprise birthday party is OK, but no one should ever ask them to keep kisses or touches secret.
- Buy your children a Travelcard and/or Phonecard so that they can always call you or get home.
- Arrange to have a family codeword. Tell your child that if anyone ever tries to collect them for you, the person will always know the codeword. 'No Code, No Go.'
- When visiting public places (shopping centres, funfairs) always arrange a meeting place with your child in case you get separated ('I will meet you outside Marks & Spencer' or 'by the fountain').
- Most paedophiles are not strangers. Tell children that if anyone, even someone they know, touches them in a confusing or frightening way they should tell you.

Tell your children

- To be wary of public toilets and to go in with a friend, if possible. If anyone approaches you, get out fast. (Parents – don't be embarrassed to stand outside the toilet and shout in 'Are you all right in there?' It puts paedophiles right off!)
- If someone you don't know speaks to you, pretend you haven't heard and walk quickly away.
- Never take sweets, presents, or lifts from people you don't know.
- Never go up to a car to give directions – keep away so that no one can get hold of you and you can run away.
- If something bad does happen to you, even if you have broken a rule, you should tell me about it and I will help sort things out.

(One child was walking in a park when told not to and was molested – she was afraid to tell because she had broken the rule about being in the park.)

Children should make a fuss!

- If someone tries to touch or grab you, shout 'NO', get away as fast as you can and then tell an adult.
- Practise the KIDSCAPE rule: 'Yell, Run, Tell'.
- Remember, if someone frightens you, it is okay to break rules, shout or make a fuss.
- Always run towards shops or places with people.
- If you think that you are being followed, go into a shop or knock on the door of a house – ask for help.
- Break any rule to keep safe. Even break a window to attract attention, if necessary.

Play safe

- Never play in dark or lonely places, or in empty streets and stairwells.
- Stay with friends or with a group and don't wander off on your own, even if you're playing hide and seek – hide with a friend.
- If you are in a shopping centre, arcade or disco and someone offers you money to do a job or errand, don't do it – it could be a trick.
- Don't walk to and from school on your own – team up with a friend or a group.
- Always tell your parents where you're going and when you'll be back.

Getting lost

- Learn your own address, telephone number and postcode.
- If you get lost, go into a shop or a place with lots of people and ask for help, or find a police officer, a security guard, or a traffic warden to ask. If you can't find a shop assistant or a person in a uniform, ask a man or a woman with children to help you.
- Don't go into a house, or office, or phonebox with anyone – wait outside while they telephone your parents or the police.
- Don't get into a car or accept a lift from anyone – say you'll wait for your parents or the police to fetch you.

Travelling alone

- Travel in a train carriage with other people.
- Carry enough money for your return trip and never spend it on anything else.
- Work out what you would do if you missed your train or bus. How would you get home? Is there someone you could call?

Telephones

- Know how to use a public call box and how to contact your parents or whoever takes care of you.
- Know how to make an emergency phone call.
- You don't need money to make a reverse charge call (the person at the other end pays the bill).
- Carry a Phonecard so that you can always call home if you get stuck somewhere.

What if something happens?

- Be aware of changes in your child's behaviour which might indicate that something is not right. (See KIDSCAPE 'Child Abuse: Signs and Symptoms' leaflet)
- If your child doesn't want to be with someone, find out why. Children may say things like, 'I don't want you to go out tonight', when they really mean 'I don't want to be left with the babysitter'.
- Stay calm and try not to transmit anger, shock or embarrassment to your child.
- Ensure that your child knows you believe him/her.
- Tell children it is NEVER their fault if someone abuses them.
- Praise your child for having told you and for 'getting through the ordeal'. Tell them you love them.
- Seek help for the child and yourself.

Free Kidscape safety guides

Child Abuse: Signs and Symptoms
Good Sense Defence for the Young
Keep Them Safe
Why My Child? Advice for parents of children who have been sexually abused

For a free copy of these safety guides or for our free anti-bullying guides and details of our books and schools safety programmes, send a large, stamped, addressed envelope to:

KIDSCAPE, 152 Buckingham Palace Road, London, SW1W 9TR. Tel: 0171 730 3300

The KIDSCAPE research study of paedophiles (sponsored by The Nuffield Foundation) is also available, upon request, from the above address.

KIDSCAPE is the only national charity teaching children about keeping safe before they become victims of abuse or bullying. KIDSCAPE'S message is prevention.

* Two-year study of paedophiles sponsored by The Nuffield Foundation

Policing paedophiles

There are 4,000 known paedophiles in Britain and 14 officers to police them. No wonder the problem is out of control. By Nick Davies, author and investigative journalist

The Belgian Minister of Justice looked weak and depressed as he sat before the world's Press this week and tried to explain how his police officers had failed to detect Marc Dutroux, who has confessed to the serial rape and abduction of young girls.

Britain's police chiefs should breathe a sigh of relief that they do not work in Belgium.

As the authorities in Brussels struggle to survive the embarrassment of their failure, their opposite numbers in Britain know that they, too, are hopelessly ill-equipped to deal with the paedophile threat.

Consider two figures. First, there are more than 4,000 names on the paedophile database which is held by the National Crime Intelligence Service (NCIS); names of men who have an established interest in the sexual abuse of children. They have been caught smuggling child pornography, buying it, selling it or are implicated in its production.

Second, there are only 14 police officers in the UK who are dedicated to catching them. To put it another way, known paedophiles outnumber the detectives by about 300 to one.

I have investigated the activities of paedophiles in Britain, Europe and the Far East. I have seen them using children for pornography, prostitution and their own casual pleasure.

Punished

The problem is unmeasured but it is certainly vast. The few detectives who deal with it know that they are losing. And their bosses know it, too, though they have done almost nothing to help.

The central difficulty is that the victims of child abuse are almost always silent. Belgian police have admitted that when they twice searched the home of 39-year-old builder Dutroux last winter, the two eight-year-old girls they were looking for almost certainly heard the search but stayed silent in their basement dungeon for fear of being punished. They subsequently starved to death.

It is a grim image and a symbol of a child's reaction to rape: because they are frightened and confused, because they have been tricked and feel guilty, they will say nothing.

This silence is particularly dangerous in the world of policing in the Nineties. Police chiefs now run their forces like businesses. They have to justify their budgets and they do this by clearing up reported crime.

On the rare occasions when child abuse is reported, they will investigate – and most forces have Juvenile Protection Units to do so. But a modern police chief is reluctant to jeopardise his budget by asking his officers to dig up a mass of unreported crime.

It is ten years since police in Kilburn, London, received a complaint of child abuse and decided to investigate not just the one allegation, but all of the secondary allegations which they found along the way. They ended up with no fewer than 653 complaints of paedophilia and charged 20 adults with serious offences against children.

The two officers who ran the Kilburn case, Roger Gaspar and John Lewis, quite reasonably wondered what would happen if every force followed up each allegation in the way they had. They were staggered by the scale of the problem they had uncovered and wrote an internal document in which they pointed out that almost all of Scotland Yard's specialist squads were devoted to protecting property.

They asked for a squad to protect children, that would gather intelligence on paedophiles and then target them to find evidence to justify arrests.

The detectives presented their paper to the Association of Chief Police Officers and to those in charge of serious crime at Scotland Yard, but it was rejected.

Three years later, Iain Donaldson, who ran the Obscene Publications Squad (OPS) from 1985 to 1989, mounted exactly the same argument in a formal proposal, entitled: 'The investigation of multiple offences of child exploitation outside the family'. That report was rejected, too.

In 1994, Michael Hames, who took over the OPS, submitted a confidential report to the Commissioner, Sir Paul Condon, arguing the same line.

Abuse

'We need a pro-active national squad to go out and gather information and to target these people like they do for burglars and robbers,' he told me then. However, his report was rejected.

Since then, there has been one advance. Scotland Yard has at last established the Paedophilia and Child Pornography Unit, which contains the only 14 officers in the country who are working full-time on the problem.

A few other cities have vice squads but they must deal with the whole range of prostitution, pimping and pornography. The paedophiles have to take their place in the queue. In most of the country's forces, there is not even a single officer attempting to detect child abuse.

Compare that with the number of specialist detectives who work on reported crimes of burglary or theft.

Remember Operation Orchid in the Eighties, when police broke a paedophile ring which had murdered four young boys from the East End of London?

At the end of that inquiry, detectives released the names of six other missing boys who they feared might also have been victims. And, unofficially, they admitted that they knew there were up to a dozen members of the ring who had escaped prosecution.

And listen to Detective Superintendent Ed Williams, who trapped the two paedophiles who abducted ten-year-old Daniel Handley from the East End and left his body in a shallow grave near Bristol. 'We are not doing enough on paedophiles,' he told me.

Offenders

When Williams started to investigate Daniel's disappearance, he discovered the files on Operation Orchid had been mislaid.

When he checked the NCIS database on paedophiles, he found its details were hopelessly out of date. When he tried to check the files of known sex offenders in the General Registry, he found that more than 30 per cent of them were nowhere to be found.

As social pressures generate more and more child abuse, the police are in danger of being left behind

When he turned to the Scientific Intelligence Unit, which is supposed to analyse evidence from all the sex crimes in London, he discovered that it consisted of only one officer and a secretary.

'It is outrageous,' he said. 'It is almost as though guys like me, and Hames and Gaspar, are seen as nuisance value to the police service.

'Child protection is not macho. Those who are involved in it are looked at askance by Met police officers. They don't have the same status as the Regional Crime Squad or Flying Squad.'

Like others before him, Ed Williams last year submitted an internal report warning of the immense danger from paedophiles, and calling for a new nation-wide offensive to build on the success of the Paedophile and Child Pornography Unit. Like the others, his report was rejected.

All these officers spoke out after they had retired from the police. None had anything to gain from doing so. But their argument is overwhelming.

As social pressures generate more and more child abuse, the police are in danger of being left behind. The tragic consequences have already become clear, first in Gloucester and now in Belgium.

Over 1,000 sex offenders fail to register with police

By Ian Burrell

Police chiefs admitted more than 1,000 of Britain's most dangerous sex offenders were missing from the register created to track their movements. Figures by the Association of Chief Police Officers (Acpo) show 1,159 of the 4,524 offenders required to register with police have not signed up. Up to 500 of those missing from the list may have 'gone to ground'.

But an Acpo spokeswoman said nearly all those not accounted for were in jail or in the 12-day period of grace after being released from custody. 'We have now got 88 per cent compliance and we regard that rate as pretty good.'

Harry Fletcher, assistant general secretary of the National Association of Probation Officers, said: 'I am sure the police and probation service will make tracking them down a priority . . . but even if they do the register will only be a fraction of the sex offenders. The total number of men living in England and Wales convicted of sex offences against women and children is 110,000.'

Nightmare on any street

Newspapers are outing paedophiles and their homes are consequently being firebombed. Do child molesters deserve a second chance after they have served their sentences? Or has the public the right to know when such a menace moves in next door? Owen Bowcott and Erlend Clouston report

Jesse Timmendequas was back in the dock in New Jersey yesterday. He is a convicted paedophile and one of the most widely reviled figures to come before an American jury; and he is fighting for his life.

The thrice-convicted sex offender faces the death penalty by lethal injection. Timmendequas's crime – which echoed round the world – was the 1994 murder of Megan Kanka, aged seven.

Timmendequas had invited his young neighbour into his home to see a new puppy. She did not emerge alive. Pieces of her clothing were found in his rubbish. A bite mark on his hand was identified as sign of her desperate last struggle.

But it was not the horror of the offence which created the headlines. Megan's mother was determined to prevent such crimes reoccurring. Her emotive, high-profile lobbying sparked off a crusade which led to the passing of both state and federal versions of what has come to be known as Megan's Law.

In essence, the regulations require local communities across the United States to be informed when a potentially dangerous sex offender is released into the neighbourhood. If parents were aware where the danger lay, the argument went, they could warn their youngsters to stay away.

The relevance to Britain of Timmendequas' sentencing was brought sharply into focus yesterday by the case of Graham Seddon. His imminent release has posed the question feared by millions of parents: how would you like to live next door to a convicted paedophile?

The 43-year-old was detained by officers in Huyton earlier this month, carrying a bag containing toys and books. He was on the lookout for a child, he readily admitted to officers. Charged with a breach of the peace, he is in a Liverpool hospital being assessed by psychiatrists and is likely to be classified as untreatable. The police will have no alternative but to order his release.

Seddon, described as an 'incredibly dangerous man' by Det Chief Inspector Paul Evans of Merseyside Police, had changed his name from Graham Stridgeon by deed poll on his release. He created a new identity, it appears, in order to erase his record and evade official surveillance.

In this country sensitivity over a released offender's civil liberties may be more keenly felt than in America, but the anger is just the same. Burnt out of their homes, refused council tenancies, hounded by vigilantes, publicly shamed by local newspapers and soon to be required to report every change of address to the police – the climate for paedophiles is one of sub-zero tolerance.

The unrepentant sex molester who snatches young children off the streets has become the bogey figure lurking behind the latest moral panic. No one has devised a reliable scheme to prevent paedophiles reoffending. Nobody wants them living anywhere near their backyard.

Yesterday's promise by the Home Office minister, Alun Michael, that there will be 'no hiding place for paedophiles' underscores the urgent attention the issue is being given by the new government.

'We intend to move fast,' Michael declared. 'There will be cases where the public will have to be told directly that a paedophile is in their area. Several frightening cases in recent months have hammered it home that we must act.'

Estimated male population in 1993 with a conviction for a sexual offence

The table below shows that 125,000 men aged 20 or over had a conviction for an offence that would have been registrable had the Sex Offenders Act been in force when they were convicted.

Age in 1993	Population	Sexual Offence				Offence against child			
		Any		Registerable		Any		Registerable	
		%	No.	%	No.	%	No.	%	No.
20 to 24	1,933,000	0.3	6,000	0.2	5,000	0.2	4,000	0.2	3,000
25 to 29	2,152,000	0.6	13,000	0.4	7,000	0.3	6,000	0.3	6,000
30 to 34	2,032,000	1.1	22,000	0.6	12,000	0.5	10,000	0.5	9,000
35 to 39	1,744,000	1.4	24,000	0.7	12,000	0.6	11,000	0.6	10,000
40 or more	10,695,000	1.8	192,000	0.8	88,000	0.7	79,000	0.7	73,000
Estimated totals	18,556,000		260,000		125,000		110,000		100,000

Source: Home Office Research and Statistics Directive

The unrepentant sex molester who snatches young children off the streets has become the bogey figure lurking behind the latest moral panic

The immediate trigger for action is the Sex Offenders Act. Passed in the dying days of John Major's administration, it established a register of all convicted paedophiles. The act requires them to inform the police of their addresses and notify the police whenever they move.

Exactly how the register will function – who will have access, whose names will be on the computer files, who will be warned – has yet to be resolved. So far the professionals and the politicians are convinced that publishing open lists would be a recipe for disaster.

A lynch law mentality would develop, the police have warned. Just how serious the threat of mob reaction to paedophiles can be was shown at the weekend on an Aberdeen council estate.

Boarded-up windows on the Middlefield estate indicate where the city's anti-paedophile vigilantes had been active. In a doorway near one of the targeted council houses, there was an air of triumph yesterday. The two brothers who lived there had deserved eviction by any means, neighbours believed.

Locals claimed that nobody in the local authority had done anything about the presence of alleged paedophiles on the estate until residents had taken the initiative them-selves. 'I wanted them out for my grand-children's sake,' explained 48-year-old Catherine Crombie.

But what if they were innocent? 'I'll swear on her life, they're not,' she snorted, gesticulating at her year-old granddaughter.

Paedophilia's capacity to destablise communities in a way not seen since the heretic-hunting of the 17th and 18th centuries has been amply demonstrated in Aberdeen over the past six days.

On Wednesday evening, a community meeting on Seaton estate, three miles from Middlefield, was told wrongly that a child molester had been rehoused in a council flat opposite a local school. The next morning dozens of placard-waving mothers demonstrated outside the address. Stones were thrown and windows broken but the tenant, 25-year-old James Wotherspoon, who has been put on six months' probation for throwing a child at his mother, had escaped the previous evening.

Two days later, another mob of men and women surrounded the flats in Logie Place and Logie Avenue. Again, the occupants managed to leave before trouble erupted. One theory is that someone saw a Wotherspoon lookalike in the area, put two and two together and made five. Grampian police were adamant yesterday that neither of the residents had a history of abusing women or children or were being investigated for any such crimes.

'These men are innocent victims of a malicious campaign,' said a police spokeswoman. This was greeted with scorn on the estate. 'Who are you going to believe, the police or the kids?' complained a pony-tailed woman.

The fury and emotions stirred up by such cases and their potential to slip into disaster has become evident in the last few years. In May 1994, a girl aged 14 called Samantha Pennell died after the house in which she had been staying was burnt down. Those who set fire to the building were looking for a paedophile, Dennis Butlin.

The following year, Lawrence Leydon, a convicted paedophile, was stabbed to death in his home in Edinburgh. Earlier this year Francis Duffy, aged 67, was badly beaten by a gang in Manchester who mistook him for Brindley Dummett, a paedophile named three months previously by the *Manchester Evening News*. Since then the cases have multiplied and several local authorities have won the right to evict convicted paedophiles from council accommodation.

The pressure from housing estates for public outings of paedophiles has so far been resisted. Paul Cavadino, principal officer of the National Association for the Care and Resettlement of Offenders, believes it would be counter-productive.

'Public outing increases the risk that paedophiles will go to ground, change their names and move around from one place to another,' he says. 'It will be more difficult to supervise them in treatment programmes.

'The evidence in the US is that Megan's Law hasn't reduced the rate of child sex offences. What we need is legislation to provide all sex offenders leaving prison with an extended period of supervision on release. If they don't co-operate then they can be reimprisoned.' Such provisions would have ensured that the legal dilemma over Graham Seddon's case might never have arisen.

The real issue, Cavadino believes, on outing is therefore how many organisations will be allowed access to the register on paedophiles. Should the Boy Scouts troop be able to check a new leader's record? Ought churches be permitted to snoop into a Sunday school teacher's background?

Rob Hutchinson, of the Association of Directors of Social Services (ADSS), is convinced that it must be left to the experts to decide who should be warned about the presence of a paedophile. Social workers, probation officers and police must assess the risks in each individual case.

'I don't think we can provide the information [on paedophiles] to people outside the normal channels,' he concludes. A joint submission by ADSS, chief police and probation officers, is due to arrive at the Home Office soon.

Liberty, the civil rights group which has monitored the implications of the Sex Offenders Act, accepts the need for some form of register. 'What we are worried about is that the government will put everyone involved in any kind of [sex] offence on the register,' says John Wadham, Liberty's director. 'Some are "one-off" which are deeply regretted and never repeated.'

In the States, Megan's Law has run into a barrage of legal challenges. The new Labour government may be after action headlines by promising immediate change; but the lesson from abroad, and from besieged bail hostels, is that there is no easy solution to one of the most insidious of crimes.

In Australia, publication of *The Australian Paedophile and Sex Offender Index*, did not lead to a rash of arson attacks across the country, though it was widely criticised as being ineffective and dangerous.

The Home Office minister Alun Michael clearly has less ambitious plans. 'Judging when the public should be given information will not be easy,' he admits. 'But the clearer the danger, the easier it is to decide.' If a known paedophile moved in with a woman who had young children, for example, she would have to be told.

Amid all the confusion about the conflicting rights of offenders to rehabilitation and the public to protection, a new proposal is being floated. The Home Office this week hinted at indefinite life sentences for paedophiles.

'Exposing the guilty is a public service'

He was in his thirties, from Biggleswade and worked outside the county. That was all the information that the *Bedfordshire on Sunday* newspaper gave about Graham Handscombe, who had been arrested though not charged for his involvement in a child porn network. In the end a coroner's court decided it was enough to help end his life.

Handscombe, they said, had taken his own life 'whilst the balance of his mind was disturbed by events which transpired from recent allegations'.

When a newspaper prints information about the identity and whereabouts of paedophiles it takes risks, says Paul Horrocks, the acting editor of the *Manchester Evening News* which has 'outed' several paedophiles. The paper must balance children's safety with the threat of mob rule; it pits the chance that a paedophile may reoffend against the fact that he has served his time and may be denied the right to resume a normal life. 'There is a risk that people will take the law into their own hands. But there is a greater risk that children will be hurt. If you can't take risks to protect children, then when can you?' he says.

One of those 'outed' by the *Manchester Evening News* suffered physical and verbal abuse from his neighbours and moved away as a result. Horrocks describes as 'regrettable' a case of mistaken identity in which an innocent man was attacked by an angry mob.

'We have never urged anybody to take the law into their own hands ... All newspapers have a duty to both reflect the views of their readers and also to do what they think is right. We think this is the right thing to do,' he says.

The *Birmingham Evening Mail* twice published the address of George Taylor and his 81-year-old mother. Taylor, who had served a three-month sentence, was released without conditions. Each time they published his address both he and his mother were forced to move on and their homes were wrecked. The *Mail*'s editor, Peter Freeman, says they would do the same again. 'It is a public service to expose paedophiles who conceal their past offences.'

In some cases newspapers have become the self-appointed monitors of paedophiles in their area. At the *Bournemouth Daily Echo* they keep a record of all those who have been convicted in their area from court reports and clippings. They are then entered on to a register which is made available to between 40 and 50 local groups which work with children.

It is the paper itself which draws up the register, vets those who wish to belong to it and then dispenses the information. They also have a policy on paedophiles coming into the area.

'A while ago we were given a tip-off that a convicted paedophile was coming into the area. We would not publicise that information. We actually sat on it until the community itself found out and responded and then we covered their response,' says Andy Martin, the *Echo*'s deputy news editor.

The problem with all of this, says Howard Lockwood, chief executive of North East London Probation Services, is that the challenge of balancing care and control has been usurped by a culture of blame. Putting ex-offenders at the mercy of mob rule, he says, often only drives them underground elsewhere.

'Public outing increases the risk that paedophiles will go to ground, change their names and move around from one place to another'

Children's right to sex, by sociologist

By Steve Doughty

Society should consider whether children should have the right to consent to sex, a conference of 600 leading academics will be told today.

Sociologist Matthew Waites will also present a rundown of the arguments of paedophiles who suggest sex between adults and children is harmless and banning it denies youngsters their 'sexual citizenship'.

Mr Waites, a doctoral student at South Bank University in London, will tell the British Sociological Association conference in York that the increasing acceptance of equal rights for homosexuals 'leads to a difficult question of children's sexuality'.

He also says in a paper: 'We live in a society which is prepared to hold two ten-year-old boys accountable as adults in adult courts for the murder of James Bulger.

'Society, it would seem, sees fit to hold under-16s responsible for crime, but will not grant them the right to consent to sexual acts, to govern their own bodies.

'There is confusion at the heart of our conceptions of the shift from childhood innocence to adult responsibility and citizenship. Are we imposing responsibilities upon children without rights?'

Turning from sex between under-16s to sex between children and adults, he says the sexual liberation movement of the Sixties and Seventies had challenged 'all existing social norms'.

He adds: 'Advocates of inter-generational sex argued that if children like sexual activity with adults, why should others interfere?

'They claimed children need not have total awareness of every ramification of their sexual acts with adults in order to give meaningful consent, precisely because what they were doing was so harmless.'

He adds that since the Sixties 'paedophile groups made their claims in terms of children's rights, arguing that their ability to consent and make decisions over their own emotions and bodies should be respected'.

His paper is certain to trigger anger. Valerie Riches, of Family and Youth Concern, said yesterday: 'The sexual rights movement is a movement towards the legalisation and acceptance of paedophilia.

'This paper is an attempt to make paedophilia academically acceptable, and that is the prelude to a political campaign for legalisation.'

Controversial scenes in the children's series *Love Bites* may be cut out following a barrage of complaints.

After the *Daily Mail* highlighted viewers' outrage at explicit scenes in last weekend's show, Liam Hamilton, director of broadcasting at London Weekend Television, said he would change next Saturday's edition if necessary.

'We are looking at the next two programmes in the light of what has been said,' he added. And he said anything 'particularly sensitive' could be cut out.

Mr Hamilton said he thought *Love Bites* as a series was 'very good' and that Saturday's programme – which featured foreplay and teenagers in intimate situations – had not breached Independent Television Commission guidelines.

The Broadcasting Standards Commission will discuss complaints about the programme next Monday before deciding whether to investigate.

Sexual offences against a child

The graph below shows the numbers and proportions who had a convicion by each age for an offence against a child. Of men born in 1953, 0.7% had a conviction by age 40 for an offence that clearly had a child victim. These made up the majority of serious sexual offences. A much larger proportion had a conviction for an offence with a girl victim than with a boy victim (0.6% and 0.1% respectively by age 40 – not illustrated).

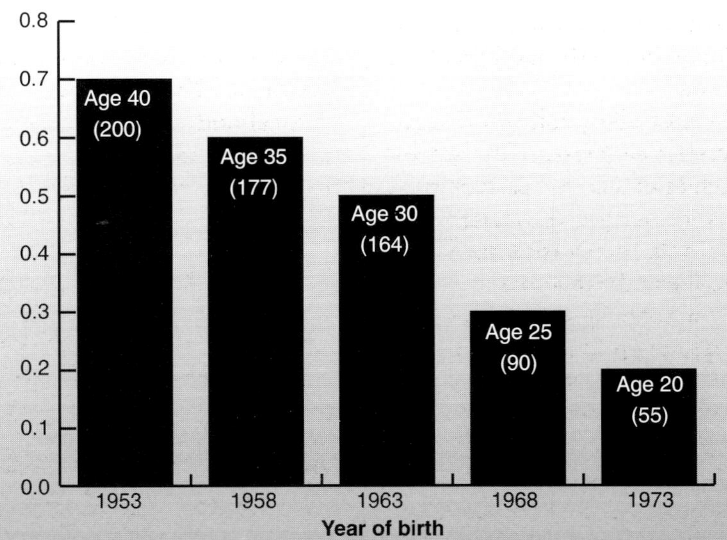

() Figures in parentheses show number convicted of these offences in each cohort at the age of 1993

Source: Home Office Research and Statistics Directorate

Moral outrage or mob rule?

As public awareness of sexual abuse increases, so does society's indignation at the crimes of paedophiles, particularly when they are released into the community. So incensed are some parents that they are forming 'lynch mobs' to drive convicted offenders out. David Mitchell reports on the rise of vigilante groups and their effect on the debate about how best to protect children

Talk about vigilantes, and American images of lynch mobs and the Ku Klux Klan spring to mind. But it is happening right here, in more prosaic places like Aberdeen, Birmingham and Liverpool, and the targets are convicted sex offenders.

Hounding sex offenders is not new, but since the beginning of the year there has been a steady spate of incidents of 'mob rule', where groups of angry mothers have taken to the streets to oust a convicted paedophile from their communities.

Why this should be happening now is not clear, but it seems to result from a combination of factors. Public awareness of sexual abuse is higher than it has ever been, spurred on by intense media coverage of tragedies like Dunblane, the Fred West case and the children's home scandals in North Wales.

There also appears to be something of a moral panic, fanned by the failures of authorities in some cases to stop paedophiles who have been released into the community from reoffending. People seem to have lost confidence in the system and have decided to take the law into their own hands.

Meanwhile, news has been filtering through from the United States about what has become known as Megan's Law, now on the statute books in most states, where communities are notified about convicted sex offenders living in their areas. If it's good enough for the United States, why not here?

It all began in Stirling, where a convicted paedophile was twice hounded from hostels after a council warning to local schools was leaked.

The mob's ringleader, 'Big Mags' Haney, became something of a folk hero after offering her services to other communities fearful of paedophiles. Since then, there have been protests throughout the country, notably in Liverpool, Birmingham and Aberdeen, where false rumours led to two council houses being vandalised and two innocent men being forced to flee.

Child abuse expert Ray Wyre, principal adviser to the Faithfull Foundation which gives treatment to sex offenders, warns that if mob rule is allowed to continue, there could be an offenders' backlash. 'If we as a society don't get hold of this problem there are dangers that we will end up with more Dunblanes. We will be setting people up with no hope and no purpose, and the danger is what they might do in this state,' he says.

'Because of the statutory agencies' failure to deal with people like Thomas Hamilton, people are taking the law into their own hands, and suddenly it's become open season. If we don't introduce legislation that will deal with this problem properly, we are going to have more and more of this behaviour, and it is not just offenders who are being targeted, it is their parents and their children.'

> ***Hounding sex offenders is not new, but since the beginning of the year there has been a steady spate of incidents of 'mob rule'***

David Niven, chairperson of Action on Child Exploitation (ACHE), believes sensational media coverage has fixed the issue as a problem in people's minds. 'If anything is guaranteed to trigger a knee-jerk response, it is children or animals in danger,' he said.

Niven says that through 'stranger-danger' messages, society almost appears to sanction law-breaking.

'People have enormous sympathy for what you're doing,' he adds.

ACHE believes its call for suspected abusers to be included in the new register of sex offenders could go some way towards allaying public fears. 'But that is only part of it. We need to look at how we get more cases to court, how they are tested there, and more child-friendly courts. It is a scandal that such a small percentage of abuse cases ever reaches the courts,' says Niven.

'There also needs to be a total revision of aspects of prevention, therapy, intervention and the criminal justice system, as well as examining how the media present images and stories of children.'

Paul Cavadino, principal officer for the National Association for the Care and Resettlement of Offenders, believes the mobs were born out of straightforward fear combined with scapegoating by more violent elements in the community. 'Recent vigilante attacks show what a complete disaster the Megan's Law approach would be here.' Cavadino says. 'When people fear attack or eviction because their identities have been disclosed, they go to ground.'

'The public is better protected if offenders are in stable accommodation, and the authorities know where they are, so they can provide some degree of supervision. It is important that the information in the register stays in the hands of the police and relevant statutory agencies.'

According to Scottish criminal justice organisation Sacro, the agenda has shifted towards community safety, focusing on the rights of the public and potential victims. 'What we are seeing reflects the fact that notions of community or society responsibility have largely gone out of the window. Individuals are seen as responsible for their own actions, and this has been taken to extremes,' says director of operations Tony Homer.

'It would be foolish to deny that there is an issue of trust. Social work departments have to go out of their way to convince the public their work with sex offenders is effective, rigorous and monitored. Unless you address the need for supervision and support, you will not significantly heighten public safety.'

John Wadham, director of civil liberties campaign group Liberty, says people quite rightly don't want sex offenders living in their streets. But injustice inevitably results sooner or later if they are identified to neighbours.

'People who have been convicted but are not in any sense a threat to children are hounded out of their homes,' he says. 'There is a moral panic about sex offenders, some of it justified in cases where they pose a real threat, but some not. We need to make sure we have a rational policy that is driven by child protection, as well as everyone's respective rights, rather than one generated by media concerns and moral panic.'

Rob Hutchinson, spokesperson for the Association of Directors of Social Services, believes the protests have more to do with the public perception of sex offenders, rather than the professionals who deal with them. 'They are saying public

protection arrangements are not sufficient to cope, and are taking the law into their own hands, but it is more likely to be an emotive, subjective reaction to the problem, rather than to the agencies themselves,' he says.

Hutchinson says there should be agreement between agencies about sharing information on paedophiles and other offenders so a proper plan can be drawn up to ensure individuals and communities are safeguarded as much as possible.

'These would be protocols between the police, social services, education and housing on risk assessment, how it is undertaken, options for sharing that information and, if necessary, action to safeguard individuals or communities,' he says.

'We are currently working with chief probation officers and chief constables to identify how those inter-agency groupings would work, what the risk assessments would look like and, most importantly, what the options for action might be.'

Terry Thomas, senior lecturer in social work at Leeds Metropolitan University, has closely studied Megan's Law and co-written a Home Office booklet on the US experience, to be published in the autumn. He believes our traditional deference to professionals has been eroded, but not by much. While professionals are being challenged more, this is still not at the level it is in the United States, which has a more aggressive democracy.

'Some UK groups are fairly ad hoc and disorganised and there hasn't been much of an attack on professionals. In the US, groups are well-organised and political, whereas in the UK they tend to be more on the streets,' he says. 'It may be moral panic playing itself out and we have seen the worst. When registers are introduced, the police say they can, on occasion, disclose information. But they will largely keep it to themselves, as will social services and probation, and they are going to hold that line.'

'Vigilante mobs are not the answer'

Mother of three Pauline Thomson founded Scottish People Against Child Abuse after the incidents on the Raploch estate in Stirling.

Thomson represents a more rational response to the problem of sex offenders in the community. She broke from vigilante leader Mags Haney after being horrified at the mob's behaviour.

SPACA is calling for a Royal Commission into the level of organised sexual abuse and an effective monitoring system for convicted sex offenders. It also wants to see a 24-hour victim support network and a register of all people working with children.

- 'Vigilante mobs are not the answer, although I understand how they feel. If vigilantes start ruling our communities, people are likely to become more frightened of them than of the perpetrators of abuse,' Thomson says.

- 'If we are going to provide a safe environment for our children, there should be more money for rehabilitation. Perpetrators should not be released into the community if they pose a danger or a threat to children.'

- 'There should be more community education and development, so that people feel more comfortable with the issues and don't start to take the law into their own hands. It will be better for us all.'

If a paedophile is my neighbour, I want to know

Are the child-abusers who claim they have been 'hounded' pushing justice to dangerous limits? By Philip Norman

A test case is being heard in the High Court this week which will strike dread into the heart of every parent. Two convicted paedophiles who were 'outed' by North Wales police are claiming legal redress for invasion of their privacy.

The plaintiffs are a man and a woman, formerly married, who were released from prison a year ago after each serving seven years of an 11-year sentence for sexual offences, mostly committed against their own children. In the next seven months, they were forced to move home three times – amid outrage of parents in the districts – after their identities were made public.

Their third place of residence was a caravan site in Wrexham, North Wales, where the site owner asked them to leave after police had shown him Press reports about their offences. The couple – now living in a caravan in a lay-by – have been given legal aid to challenge the police action.

Their counsel, Stephen Solley QC, has told the High Court that they have been treated 'unjustifiably, unreasonably and unlawfully', and that being hounded from place to place prevents them from receiving medical treatment or therapy. The couple have become outlaws under the ancient definition of 'being deprived of the benefit of the law and of the king's protection'.

It is only fitting that the Lord Chief Justice, Lord Bingham, and his fellow judge Mr Justice Buxton, be asked to determine one of the most vexed questions of modern times. To what extent should our zeal to shield our children from abuse be balanced by the recognition that child-abusers still have inalienable rights under the law?

We are all thankful to live in a country not governed by mass hysteria, vigilante justice and mob rule. The old-fashioned euphemism for prison is a 'debt to society' which, once discharged, allows the debtor to begin again with a clean slate.

Most of us abhor the idea of blacklists and denouncing people behind their backs as despicable manifestations of old-style communism and would feel deeply uneasy if the police were to take on such a role in any other context.

But this is not any other context. This is child abuse – the infliction of disgusting indignities upon those whose innocence it should be the paramount duty of any civilised society to protect. And, as a parent myself, I am deeply uneasy to see what has become a familiar metamorphosis of predators into victims.

The couple – who for legal reasons cannot be named – could hardly have chosen worse places in which to seek anonymity. The second place where they attempted to settle was Colwyn Bay, North Wales, about a mile from the seaside resort of Llandudno. It was in Llandudno, just a year ago, that seven-year-old Sophie Hook was raped and murdered after being abducted from a tent in her uncle's garden.

Proof of the times in which we live is that details of this horrific crime are already hazy. For paedophilia, once an aberration in British society, has turned into an epidemic. Each week seems to bring a new example that evokes incredulity as much as horror and disgust. We are inured to the idea of rampant child abuse in schools and children's homes.

We have adjusted our mental picture of paedophiles – no longer maladjusted male misfits in raincoats but, possibly, a married couple like

the present plaintiffs who abused their children under the cover of an apparently normal home.

We have accepted – there being no other choice – that the tides of glossy brutality that wash out of film and television screens have brought thousands of susceptible minds to a horribly synchronised breaking point. We have accepted that a whole new race of monsters stalk this country's streets, watching and waiting for any child in any place to take a few unguarded steps alone.

Monsters are what these people are, or have become. What other description can there be of someone who uses adult guile to befriend a little girl or boy, to win their trust, sexually abuse them and then, in inexplicable frenzies of rage or self-hatred, take their life?

Yes, there are always circumstances to be advanced in mitigation – that the abuser himself was once the victim of terrible cruelty. Yes, it is possible for enforced therapy to do some good and for some abusers to emerge from prison cured of their perversion and able to lead normal lives once more. But we know that in too many cases no such redemption takes place and that uncured or unrepentant paedophiles are part of the pathetic, dangerous human flotsam that swills around Britain under the awful Thatcherite misnomer 'care in the community'.

Social workers, by and large, are against the 'outing' policy that has been adopted by many police forces, often with the co-operation of local newspapers. They believe it is far better for social services to be able to keep tabs on individual paedophiles and continue the rehabilitation process. Driving them underground is potentially far more dangerous.

But no responsible parent can possibly go along with this. In a world where so many unknown dangers menace our children, we must demand to be forewarned of every possible known one. The people who have demonstrated against these – and other – sex-offenders 'in the community' are not vigilantes or lynch mobs but ordinary, decent mothers and fathers no longer confident that officialdom cares more for the law-abiding than for the law-breaker.

The case currently being heard in the High Court could have implications for this urgent right to know. If the court decides the North Wales police acted illegally in 'outing' the couple, it will affect Home Office guidelines, now being drawn up, which would make information about sex-offenders available to schools, youth clubs etc. in their area. It had been hoped to finalise these guidelines by the autumn when the Sex Offenders Act, giving police statutory rights in the disclosure of information, becomes law.

For the two paedophiles, their QC has argued that police action infringed their rights under Section 8 of the European Convention on Human Rights, which provides that everyone has a right to 'respect for his private and family life, his home and his correspondence'.

Agreed. But I would place much higher the rights of a child to walk the street, free from fear of monsters. And I would leave the two plaintiffs to stew in their lay-by. For that, ultimately, was their choice.

250,000 men are known sex offenders

By Philip Johnston , Home Affairs Editor

More than 250,000 men over 20 have been convicted of a sex offence, according to Home Office figures to be published today.

Of these, the crimes of 125,000 were serious enough to require registration with the police under laws introduced in the last Parliament.

At least 110,000 had been convicted for an offence against a child, of which 100,000 would need to be included on the new national register, 15 per cent of them for life.

The Home Office research directorate findings will show that about one in 60 men born in 1953 had a conviction for a sex offence by the age of 40. At least 10 per cent of these offended again within five years.

It is the first time information has been available giving a reliable estimate of the numbers of known sex offenders. Figures are normally produced on an annual basis showing conviction rates for the year.

At least 110,000 had been convicted for an offence against a child, of which 100,000 would need to be included on the new national register

In 1995 there were 4,600 convictions and 2,200 cautions of men for a serious sex offence. There were a further 1,300 for possessing obscene material or indecent exposure.

The findings come as ministers prepare a series of measures intended to toughen the law on sex offenders.

They include giving judges the power to pass an indeterminate sentence for serious sex offenders and more effective supervision of paedophiles released from prison.

6,000 names to go on sex offenders' list next month

By Richard Ford, Home correspondent

Six thousand names will be put on the national sex offenders' register immediately it comes into effect at the beginning of next month, the Home Office said yesterday.

The names will include those of offenders convicted of sex crimes who are in jail or under probation supervision. The Home Office estimated that another 3,500 names a year would be added to the register, which will be held on the police national computer.

Because the Sex Offenders Act setting up the register does not operate retrospectively, the overwhelming majority of the 110,000 convicted paedophiles in England and Wales will escape being put on the list. Their names will be added only if they are convicted of another sex offence.

Under guidelines issued yesterday, the police will be expected to warn local communities when convicted sex offenders, including rapists, move into the neighbourhood only in exceptional circumstances. The guidance says that any decision to name an offender must be 'justified on the basis of the likelihood of the harm which non-disclosure might otherwise cause'. It said that disclosure of personal information about individual offenders should be 'exceptions to a general policy of confidentiality'.

Alun Michael, Minister of State at the Home Office, said that the guidelines were an important step in protecting the public, particularly children, from sex offenders. But, he added, the guidance was not a magic wand to the problem of dealing with sex offenders in the community.

Mr Michael said he hoped that the guidelines would end media campaigns that have identified alleged paedophiles. 'There should not be a general broadcasting of names and addresses unless the risk assessment shows that it is needed,' he said.

Under the guidelines, if an offender is living near a school, a day nursery or a playgroup, police will be able to tell the local education authority, the head teacher or the playgroup leader.

Police could also step in if an offender was helping with running a youth group by informing the church authorities or governing body.

The announcement was welcomed by the Association of Chief Police Officers. It said that decisions must be taken case by case.

Under the Sex Offenders Act, which comes into force on September 1, offenders convicted or cautioned for a range of sex offences will have to tell the police where they live and when they move. If they fail to register they face a six-month jail sentence and/or a £5,000 fine. The offences covered by the Act include rape, sexual intercourse with a girl under the age of 13, incest by a man, buggery, indecent assault between men, indecent assault on a man and assault with intent to commit buggery.

The National Association of Probation Officers said that there were serious limitations to the register. Harry Fletcher, assistant general secretary, said 'Many [paedophiles] have changed their identities on several occasions, yet the onus would be on the offender to register any change of circumstances with the police. Given the devious nature of the offending, in many instances this will not happen.'

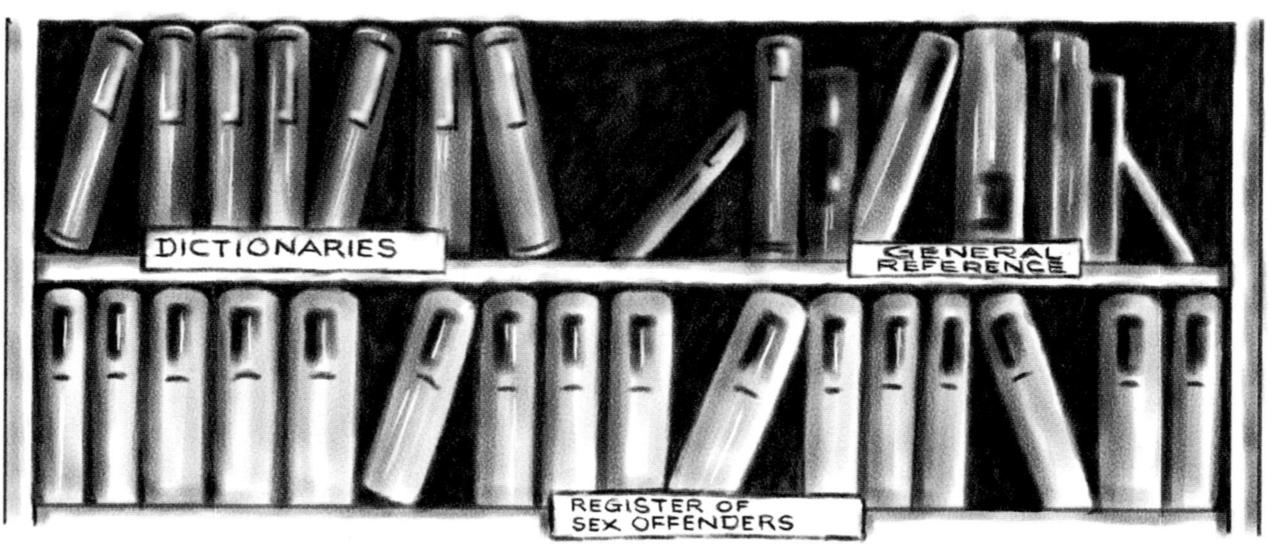

ADDITIONAL RESOURCES

You might like to contact the following organisations for further information. Due to the increasing cost of postage, many organisations cannot respond to enquiries unless they receive a stamped, addressed envelope.

Barnardo's
Tanners Lane
Barkingside
Ilford
Essex, IG6 1QG
Tel: 0181 550 8822
Fax: 0181 551 6870
Works to help each person achieve his or her potential. Produces publications.

Barnardo's (Scotland)
235 Corstorphine Road
Edinburgh, EH12 7AR
Tel: 0131 334 9893
Fax: 0131 316 4008
Offers support and information to children and their families who are threatened with abuse.

ChildLine
2nd Floor Royal Mail Building
Studd Street
London, N1 0QW
Tel: 0171 239 1000
Fax: 0171 239 1001
ChildLine is the free, national helpline for children and young people in trouble or danger, Freephone 0800 1111. It provides confidential phone counselling service for any child with any problem 24 hours a day. Produces publications.

ECPAT UK
Thomas Clarkson House
The Stableyard
Broomgrove Road
London, SW9 9TL
Web site: See page 43 for details.
Tel: 0171 924 9555
Fax: 0171 738 4110
ECPAT UK is a campaign that exists to raise awareness and call for informed action to ensure children everywhere enjoy their fundamental rights free and secure from all forms of commercial sexual exploitation, namely child prostitution, child pornography and the trafficking of children for sexual purposes. Produces publications.

EPOCH (End all Physical Punishment of Children)
77 Holloway Road
London, N7 8JZ
Tel: 0171 700 0627
Fax: 0171 700 1105
Works to end all physical punishment of children by parents and other carers through education and legal reform.

Family and Youth Concern
322 Woodstock Road
Oxford, OX2 7NS
Tel: 01865 556 848
Fax: 01865 52774
A national organisation with no political or religious affiliations. They produce leaflets, pamphlets, books, reports and video tapes on matters affecting the family.

Kidscape
152 Buckingham Palace Road
London, SW1W 9TR
Tel: 0171 730 3300
Fax: 0171 730 7081
Web site: See page 43 for details.
Works to prevent the abuse of children through education programmes involving parents and teachers. Produces a wide range of books, videos and leaflets on child-related issues including bullying and child abuse. Ask for their publications list.

National Children's Bureau
8 Wakely Street
London, EC1V 7QE
Tel: 0171 843 6000
Fax: 0171 278 9512
Provides information on children's needs in the family, school and society. They publish a series of factsheets call *Highlights* which give an overview of various issues including child abuse and bullying.

NCH Action for Children
85 Highbury Park
London, N5 1UD
Tel: 0171 226 2033
Fax: 0171 226 2537
One of the UK's leading childcare charities with 250 projects nationwide helping over 25,000 children and young people every year.

NSPCC (National Society for the Prevention of Cruelty to Children)
National Centre
42 Curtain Road
London, EC2A 3NH
Tel: 0171 825 2500
Fax: 0171 825 2525
Has a network of Child Protection Teams and projects to protect children from abuse. Can help parents, carers and relatives who feel they may be in danger of harming their children.
Operates the Child Protection Helpline offering counselling and support. Tel: 0800 800 500.

Save the Children
17 Grove Lane
London, SE5 8RD
Tel: 0171 703 5400
Fax: 0171 703 2278
Produces a wide range of materials. Ask for their catalogue.

Scottish Women's Aid
12 Torphichen Street
Edinburgh, EH3 8JQ
Tel: 0131 2210401
Fax: 0131 221 0401
Provides advice and information for women and their children who are threatened by mental, emotional or physical abuse.

INDEX

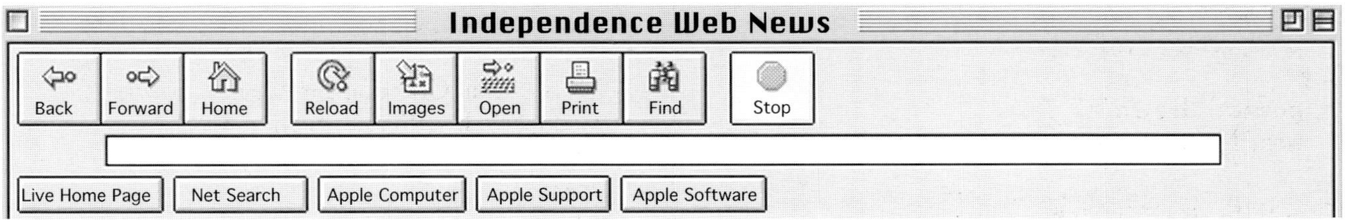

The Internet has been likened to shopping in a supermarket without aisles. The press of a button on a Web browser can bring up thousands of sites but working your way though them to find what you want can involve long and frustrating on-line searches. And unfortunately many sites contain inaccurate, misleading or heavily biased information. Our researchers have therefore undertaken an extensive analysis to bring you a selection of quality Web site addresses. If our readers feel that this new innovation in the series is useful, we plan to provide a more extensive Web site section in each new book in the ***Issues*** series.

*****

BBC Children in Need
www.access.digex.net/~issd/abuse.htm
Factual information on child abuse. Advice for children on what they can do to avoid or report neglect or ill-treatment. For adults, a list of 10 things to do to avoid hurting a child.

American Academy of Child and Adolescent Psychiatry
http://www.aacap.org/web/aacap/factsfam
Publishes an on-line series of factsheets which provide concise information on issues which affect children. There are a number of factsheets listed including No.5 *Child Abuse – The Hidden Bruises* and No. 9 *Child Sexual Abuse.*

ChildLine
http://www.childline.org.co/abuse.html
This web site outlines different forms of abuse and gives information on abusers, the effects of child abuse, what children should know and also gives quotes from children who have in the past contacted ChildLine regarding child abuse. It also gives ways of getting help for children, families and anyone concerned with this issue.

ECPAT UK
Coalition on Child Prostitution & Tourism
http://www.euro-index.co.uk/ccpt/index.htm
This site outlines the aims of the Coalition and its efforts to change legislation around the world. It describes the link between tourism and sexual/ commercial exploitation of children.

Kidscape
http://www.solnet.co.uk/kidscape/
Kidscape aims to keep children safe from abuse before they become victims. This site describes signs and symptoms of neglect and sexual, physical and emotional abuse. Advice is given on how to respond if a child tells you about abuse, and where to find help.

International Child Abuse Network
http://www.yesican.org/definitions.html
Defines four forms of child maltreatment: neglect, emotional, physical and sexual abuse, taking their definition from the Child Abuse Prevention and Treatment Act (CAPTA) of October 1996. List of articles and publications associated with child abuse.

ACKNOWLEDGEMENTS

The publisher is grateful for permission to reproduce the following material.

While every care has been taken to trace and acknowledge copyright, the publisher tenders its apology for any accidental infringement or where copyright has proved untraceable. The publisher would be pleased to come to a suitable arrangement in any such case with the rightful owner.

Chapter One: Abused Children

Child sexual abuse, © Scottish Women's Aid, *Children's problems*, © ChildLine, *Fact or fiction?*, © NSPCC, *World states tackle spiralling child sex abuse*, © The Guardian, August 1996, *Repeat offenders face 'castration'*, © The Guardian, August 1996, *If you care about children*, © NSPCC, *Sexual exploitation*, © Young People Now, February 1997, *Protecting children everywhere against commercial sexual exploitation*, © ECPAT (UK), *Why children call ChildLine*, © ChildLine, *Speaking out about abuse*, © NSPCC, *Child protection*, © NCH '98 Factfile, *Protecting children from abuse*, © Sports Council, *Out alone*, © NSPCC, *International conference says even a cuff should be outlawed*, © The Independent, August 1996, *Crimes and punishment*, © The Guardian, August 1997, *Great and good support Carey over smacking*, © Telegraph Group Limited, London 1996, *Hitting children*, © EPOCH Worldwide, *Parents' right to smack defended*, © The Independent, September 1996, *A smack today, but tearaway tomorrow*, © The Daily Mail, August 1997.

Chapter Two

Protect children from paedophiles!, © Kidscape, *Policing paedophiles*, © The Daily Mail, August 1997, *Over 1,000 sex offenders fail to register with police*, © The Independent, December 1997, *Nightmare on any street*, © The Guardian, June 1997, *Estimated male population in 1993 with a conviction for a sexual offence*, © Reproduced with the kind permission of Her Majesty's Stationery Office (HMSO), *Children's right to sex by sociologist*, © The Daily Mail, April 1997, *Proportion in five birth cohorts with a conviction at each age for a sexual offence against a child*, © Reproduced with the kind permission of Her Majesty's Stationery Office (HMSO), *Moral outrage or mob rule?*, © Community Care, August 1997, *If a paedophile is my neighbour, I want to know*, © The Daily Express, July 1997, *250,000 men are known sex offenders*, © Telegraph Group Limited, London 1997, *6,000 names to go on sex offenders' list next month*, © Times Newspapers Limited, August 1997.

Photographs and illustrations:

Pages 1, 8, 21, 29, 30, 38, 40: The Attic Publishing Co, page 6: NSPCC / Naomi Schillinger, pages 9, 20, 23, 27: Ken Pyne, pages 10, 13, 14: Larry Bray / ChildLine, page 12: Sandra Lousada / NSPCC, page 18: Duncan Ridgley / NSPCC, page 33: Anthony Haythornthwaite.

Thank you

Darin Jewell for assisting in the editorial research for this publication.

Craig Donnellan
Cambridge
April, 1998